ALLEN CARR

STOP SMOKING NOW

WITHOUT GAINING WEIGHT

ALLEN CARR

STOP SMOKING NOW

WITHOUT GAINING WEIGHT

ARCTURUS

To John Dicey in recognition of his fantastic work helping to spread
Allen Carr's Easyway throughout the world.

Editor: Robin Hayley
Additional editorial contributions: Tim Glynne-Jones

ARCTURUS
This edition published in 2015 by Arcturus Publishing Limited
26/27 Bickels Yard, 151–153 Bermondsey Street,
London SE1 3HA

ISBN: 978-1-84837-373-0
AD000040UK

Printed in the UK

ALLEN CARR

Allen Carr was a chain-smoker for over 30 years. In 1983, after countless failed attempts to quit, he went from 100 cigarettes a day to zero without suffering withdrawal pangs, without using willpower, and without putting on weight. He realized that he had discovered what the world had been waiting for – the Easy Way to Stop Smoking, and embarked on a mission to help cure the world's smokers.

As a result of the phenomenal success of his method, he gained an international reputation as the world's leading expert on stopping smoking and his network of clinics now spans the globe. His first book, *Allen Carr's Easy Way to Stop Smoking*, has sold over 12 million copies, remains a global bestseller and has been published in over 40 different languages. Hundreds of thousands of smokers have successfully quit at Allen Carr's Easyway Clinics where, with a success rate of over 90%, he guarantees you'll find it easy to stop or your money back.

Allen Carr's Easyway method has been successfully applied to a host of issues including weight control, alcohol, and other addictions and fears. A list of Allen Carr clinics appears at the back of this book. Should you require any assistance or if you have any questions, please do not hesitate to contact your nearest clinic.

For more information about Allen Carr's Easyway, please visit
www.allencarr.com

What the media say about Allen Carr's Easyway

"I was exhilarated by a new sense of freedom."
The Independent

"A different approach. A stunning success."
The Sun

"His skill is in removing the psychological dependence."
Sunday Times

"Allow Allen Carr to help you escape today."
The Observer

"Allen Carr explodes the myth that giving up smoking is difficult."
The Times

"The smoker does not feel he is depriving himself by stopping."
The Guardian

"I suffered no serious withdrawal pangs… a month later I still have no desire to smoke."
The Daily Telegraph

"Afterwards I couldn't believe that I didn't want to smoke – but I didn't…. After five months I haven't had a single cigarette!"
Sunday Express

"An intelligent and original method!"
London Evening Standard

"For the first time in my adult life I am free."
Woman's Journal

"I always thought if I didn't have the strength to stop on my own, how could anyone else help? – I can honestly say 4 months later I haven't missed cigarettes at all."
Zest magazine

"I've never been more confident about not smoking."
Tatler

"Allen Carr has helped a host of top stars quit cigarettes."
News of the World

What celebrities say about Allen Carr's Easyway

Sir Richard Branson

"His method is absolutely unique, removing the dependence on cigarettes, while you are actually smoking. I'm pleased to say it has worked for many of my friends and my staff."

Gianluca Vialli

"I stopped with an Allen Carr's Easyway to Stop Smoking Seminar. I wanted to feel free, not a slave to nicotine which does not give you any pleasure."

Sir Anthony Hopkins

"Instantly I was freed from my addiction. I found it not only easy but unbelievably enjoyable to stay stopped."

Carole Caplin

"For the past 20 years or so, I've been sending clients wishing to stop smoking to the clinics run by Britain's internationally renowned quit smoking expert, Allen Carr. Allen has a remarkably high success rate at his worldwide network of clinics... I believe it's a public health scandal that the taxpayer-funded quit smoking authorities in this and other countries don't seek Allen's advice and guidance as many major international companies do."

Ruby Wax

"It didn't take any willpower. I didn't miss it at all and I thank God every day that I am free."

Ellen DeGeneres

"I stopped smoking… I read this book by Allen Carr. It's called the Easy Way to Stop Smoking. Everyone who reads this book stops smoking!"

Ashton Kutcher

"I read this book by this guy Allen Carr and it's called The Easy Way to Stop Smoking, and the great thing is while you're reading the book you get to smoke… this guy's brilliant. And you get to the last page and he says, 'All right, light your last one,' and you're like, 'I don't know if I want it – but, OK, if you say so, Allen.' That was it and you put it out and then you're just done. And I haven't smoked since…"

Anjelica Huston

"Allen Carr's Easy Way to Stop Smoking program achieved for me a thing that I thought was not possible – to give up a thirty-year smoking habit literally overnight. It was nothing short of a miracle."

Other celebrity clients/users include: Johnny Cash, Dave Stewart, Bruce Oldfield, Julie Christie, Kerry Packer, Susannah York, Marie Helvin, Harvey Weinstein, Goldie Hawn, John Sessions, Lord & Lady Bonham Carter, Lady Astor, Leslie Grantham, Dennis Waterman, Rula Lenska, John Cougar Mellencamp, Rick Parfitt, Martin Clunes, Robson Green, Vicky Binns, George Melly, Derek Jameson, Sean Bean, Michelle Collins, Paul Whitehouse, Ross Kemp, Krishnan Guru-Murthy, Ronnie O'Sullivan, Stefano Gabbana (of Dolce & Gabbana)… and many others who wish to remain anonymous.

What doctors say about Allen Carr's Easyway

"I have observed Allen Carr's Easyway method at first hand and have found it to be very successful and I wholeheartedly support it as an effective way to quit smoking."

Dr Anil Visram B.Sc, MBBch, FRCA, Consultant, Royal Hospitals NHS Trust, Royal London Hospital

"I was really impressed by the method. In spite of the success and fame of Allen Carr's Easyway, there were no gimmicks and the professional approach was something a GP could readily respect. I would be happy to give a medical endorsement of the method to anyone."

Dr PM Bray MB, CHb, MRCGP

"I do not know of any other method which approaches the effectiveness of Allen Carr's Easyway. The success rates you achieve (between 75% and 80%) are far in excess of anything known to me or my colleagues. I will therefore happily continue to recommend Allen Carr's Easyway both professionally and personally."

Dr Ricardo Serralta Gonzalez, National Co-ordinator, Medical Services, Schweppes

"What strikes me most powerfully is that there are none of the withdrawal pangs suffered with other methods. The percentage of success achieved (80%) is extremely high."

Dr Jose Alvarez Salcedo, Head of Medical Services, Transfesa

"It is a remarkable fact that Allen Carr, on his own admission a non-professional in behaviour modification, should have succeeded where countless psychologists and psychiatrists holding postgraduate qualifications have failed, in formulating a simple and effective way to stop smoking."

Dr William Green, MB, Chb, FRANZCP, MRCPsych, DPM, Head of Psychiatric Dept, Matilda Hospital, Hong Kong

Allen Carr's Easyway

The key which will set you free

CONTENTS

INTRODUCTION

On an otherwise unremarkable afternoon in April 1989 something extraordinary happened in my life. I was a heavy smoker. I knew it was killing me and costing me a fortune. The worst thing though was that it was controlling my life. I'd tried to quit before by using willpower, nicotine gum and various other gimmicks but I was always miserable and ended up failing. I was terrified that I would never be able to enjoy meals, drinks or social occasions without a cigarette and that I wouldn't be able to cope with stress. I also dreaded the trauma I'd suffered on my previous failed attempts and feared I could never get free from the craving.

As I rang the bell at Allen Carr's unassuming home in the London suburb of Raynes Park, I wasn't confident that this was going to be any different. However, my older brother had attended a session there and claimed he found it easy to stop and didn't miss it at all. Since he had been a chain-smoker whose failed attempts to quit I had witnessed time and again, this was amazing. When around half a dozen other people I had considered confirmed smokers reported similar experiences after visiting Allen Carr, I began to think there might be hope for me and since there was a money-back guarantee, I thought: "What have I got to lose?"

The five hours I spent with Allen Carr and a group of smokers over twenty years ago changed my life. I entered that session as a smoker who had to have at least two packets on me at all times or I would panic; who was convinced that I would have to give up one of life's pleasures and would feel miserable and deprived; who was frightened that I wouldn't be able to deal with difficult situations; and who found it almost impossible to imagine a life without cigarettes. I left with no need or desire to smoke. I suffered no withdrawal pangs. Like my brother and my friends, I found it easy to stop. It took no willpower. I immediately started enjoying social occasions more and handling stress better as Allen had predicted. There was no feeling of deprivation, instead I felt huge relief and utter elation that I was free. What's more, like the others, I didn't put on any weight. It was truly extraordinary.

I realised at once that Allen Carr had devised a method that could help millions of smokers all over the world quit easily and immediately and I wrote to him asking if I could join him in his mission. It was my great good fortune that I was accepted. Allen then trained me as a therapist and we set up the second clinic together in Birmingham. Shortly afterwards I was lucky enough to be appointed Managing Director of a company formed to spread the method all over the world and my vision of a global organisation began to become a reality.

Today, over 350,000 people have visited our clinics in more than 40 countries around the world. The clinics still provide a full and genuine money-back guarantee on demand, should you not stop for at least three months. Most smokers require just one session. Fewer than 10% of all those who have attended the clinics have claimed their money back.

In addition, more than 14 million Allen Carr's Easyway books have been sold worldwide in over 40 languages, with an estimated total readership of 30–40 million people, making our publishing programme easily the most successful in the history of smoking cessation. This phenomenal success has been achieved not through advertising or marketing but through the personal recommendations of the millions of happy ex-smokers who've quit with the method. Allen Carr's Easyway has spread all over the world for one reason alone: BECAUSE IT WORKS.

You now hold in your hands the key that will set you free.

Robin Hayley M.A. (Oxon), M.B.A., M.A.A.C.T.I.
Managing Director, Allen Carr's Easyway (International) Ltd

CHAPTER 1

WHY YOU SMOKE

NICOTINE ADDICTION

Nicotine, a colourless, oily compound, is the drug contained in tobacco that addicts you to smoking. It's the fastest addictive drug known to mankind, and just one cigarette can get you hooked.

Every puff on a cigarette delivers, via the lungs to the brain, a small dose of nicotine that acts more rapidly than the dose of heroin the addict injects into his veins. If there are twenty puffs for you in a cigarette, you receive twenty doses of the drug with just one cigarette.

Nicotine is a quick-acting drug, and levels in the bloodstream fall swiftly to about half within thirty minutes of smoking a cigarette and to a quarter within an hour. This explains why most smokers average about twenty per day.

As soon as the smoker extinguishes the cigarette, the nicotine rapidly leaves and the body withdraws from the drug.

At this point I must dispel a common illusion that smokers have about withdrawal pangs. Smokers think that withdrawal pangs are the terrible trauma they suffer when they try or are forced to stop smoking. In reality, these are mainly mental – the smoker is feeling deprived of his pleasure or prop. I will explain more about this later.

The physical withdrawal from nicotine is so subtle that most smokers have lived and died without even realising they're drug addicts. When we use the term "nicotine addict" we think we just "got into the habit". Most smokers have a horror of drugs, yet that's exactly what they are – drug addicts. Fortunately it is an easy drug to kick, but you need first to accept that you're addicted.

Within seven seconds of lighting a cigarette fresh nicotine is supplied and the pangs end, resulting in the feeling of relaxation and confidence that the cigarette appears to give to the smoker.

In the early days, when we first start smoking, the withdrawal pangs and their relief are so slight that we're not even aware of their existence. When we start smoking regularly we think it's because we've either come to enjoy them or just got into the "habit". The truth is we're already hooked but don't realise it. We've created a Little Nicotine Monster inside our stomach and every now and then we have to feed it.

All smokers start smoking for stupid reasons. Nobody has to. The only reason anybody continues smoking, whether they be a casual or a heavy smoker, is to feed that Little Monster.

The greatest irony about smoking is that the enjoyment that the smoker gets from a cigarette is the pleasure of trying to get back to the state of peace, tranquillity and confidence that his body had before he got hooked in the first place. You know that feeling when a neighbour's burglar alarm has been ringing all day, or there has been some other minor, persistent aggravation. Then the noise suddenly stops and there's a marvellous feeling of peace and tranquillity, but all we're enjoying is the end of the aggravation. In reality, all any smoker is trying to do whenever they light a cigarette is to get rid of the empty, insecure feeling of the body withdrawing from nicotine which non-smokers do not suffer from anyway. In other words, we smoke in order to feel like a non-smoker.

Before we start smoking, our bodies are complete. We then force nicotine into our body, and when we put that cigarette out and the drug starts to leave, our body suffers withdrawal – not physical pain, just an empty feeling. We're scarcely even aware of it, but it's like a dripping tap inside us. Our rational mind doesn't understand it. All we know is that we want a cigarette, and when we light it the craving goes, and for the moment we're content and confident again just as we were before we got addicted. However, the satisfaction is only temporary because, in order to relieve the craving, you have to put more nicotine into the body. As soon as you extinguish that cigarette the craving starts again, and so the chain goes on. It's a chain for life – **UNLESS YOU BREAK IT.**

"I'M GOING TO CURE THE WORLD OF SMOKING!"

People have asked what qualifies me to help the world quit smoking. After all, I am neither a doctor nor a psychiatrist. I explain why no one could be better qualified

I spent 33 years as a smoker, puffing my way through as many as a hundred cigarettes a day, and never fewer than sixty. I looked and felt terrible. In addition to the chronic health problems, there was the self-loathing, the lack of self-esteem and the feeling that my life was out of control.

I had a permanent headache caused by the constant coughing; I suffered frequent and severe nosebleeds; my sinuses throbbed constantly and I feared that at any moment I could die from a brain haemorrhage. I knew it was killing me, but I still kept smoking.

I made dozens of attempts to quit. I once stopped for six months and I was still climbing the wall. It wasn't as if I enjoyed smoking; oddly enough I never suffered from that illusion. But I did think a cigarette helped me to relax. I was also convinced that it gave me courage and confidence, and I honestly believed that I couldn't be happy without one.

It seemed as if my life depended on cigarettes, and I was literally prepared to die rather than go without them. I have still not met anybody who was as badly hooked (or, rather, thought he was as badly hooked) as I was.

I am aware that when I describe the depths I had descended to, most readers, particularly younger smokers or casual smokers, will be consoling themselves with the thought: "I would never let it get to that stage, and if it did, I would stop."

I am also aware that you might be forming the impression that this book will be umpteen pages of blood and gore and that I'm going to attempt to frighten you into quitting. Not so. If I thought that I could succeed by using shock tactics, I wouldn't hesitate for a second. But thoughts like those didn't help me to stop and, if they were of any use to you, you would already be a non-smoker. On the contrary, I promise you that I have nothing but good news for you and certainly no shock tactics.

> You need to understand why smokers who are aware they're killing themselves still don't stop; because unless you do, you won't stop either!

Back in the days when I smoked, I decided to agree to my wife Joyce's plea for me to see a hypnotherapist who claimed to be able to help people quit smoking. I was certain he wouldn't be able to help me, but Joyce had made me feel guilty, and I thought that if I went through the ritual, I could come home with a clear conscience and say, "You see, it was a complete waste of time and money. Will you now just accept that, whether I like it or not, I will never be able to stop?"

In fact, these were the actual words that I greeted Joyce with on my return:

"I'M GOING TO CURE THE WORLD OF SMOKING!"

Her disbelief was understandable. She had witnessed my

countless failed attempts to stop. She remembered how I had once looked her straight in the eye and lied when I assured her that I had stopped but continued smoking behind her back. My most recent attempt two years earlier had ended in tears after months of black depression, bad temper and abject misery.

THIS TIME IT WAS DIFFERENT

What you will find difficult to believe is that, before I stubbed out my final cigarette, I was already a non-smoker and already knew that I would never have the need or desire to smoke again.

Mind you, I wasn't expecting it to be easy and it was an incredible revelation when, not only did I find it ridiculously simple, but I actually enjoyed the whole process from the moment I extinguished my final cigarette. It didn't take any willpower, I suffered no withdrawal pangs and I haven't had the slightest desire to smoke since that day. An additional bonus was that I didn't even put on weight, in fact I lost over two stone.

It's a myth that you have to gain weight when you quit. Six months after I put out my final cigarette, I was 30 pounds lighter than I had been as a smoker!

15 July 1983 was the most important day in my life, when everything suddenly fell into place, and I realised that I didn't need to smoke. It wasn't the hypnotherapy itself that did the trick, it was a point the hypnotherapist made.

At one stage he happened to say, "Smoking is an addiction." A simple statement, uttered almost in passing, yet it had never crossed my mind until then. The effect was astonishing. I didn't need to hear anything more after that; I had found the key to unlock my personal prison cell.

If smoking was just an addiction, then it lost all its power and mystique. It was not something I did for pleasure or comfort, but something I felt compelled to do to feed my addiction. There was no genetic difference between smokers and non-smokers, it was simply a trap into which anybody could fall if they succumbed to the pressure to start smoking in the first place. From that moment I knew I could get free and felt confident I could also help others to escape – forever.

> To quit successfully, you need to focus on what the cigarette is doing for you. Once you understand you're not making a sacrifice, you're well on your way to freedom.

I will explain more about hypnotherapy later and how it can be beneficial, but I can tell you now it wasn't the hypnotherapy that enabled me to succeed in quitting smoking. Although on that day I didn't comprehend the full significance of what happened to me, I was aware I had discovered something every smoker yearns for:

AN EASY WAY TO STOP SMOKING

At first I wasn't clear why previous attempts to quit had been such torture and yet this time it was the complete opposite. I kept asking myself the wrong question: why was it so easy and enjoyable to quit this time? When I asked myself why it had been such a nightmare on previous attempts, it all suddenly made sense.

The beautiful truth is: IT IS EASY TO STOP IF YOU GO ABOUT IT IN THE RIGHT WAY. Go about it the wrong way, however, and it can become VIRTUALLY IMPOSSIBLE.

I then developed a method of communicating what the right way is and tested it out on friends and relatives. The results confirmed my belief that it could work for any smoker.

So convinced was I that I took the momentous decision to leave my profession and set up a full-time clinic helping others to escape from the slavery of nicotine.

News of the method spread like wildfire by word of mouth and we soon had no need to advertise. In fact, smokers started visiting me not only from every corner of the UK but also flying in from all over the world, solely because of the personal recommendations they had received from successful clients.

When we could no longer treat the number of smokers seeking our help, I set out the method in a book, *The Easy Way To Stop Smoking*. The book is a global hit and by the far the best-selling book on smoking ever published, with translations in over 40 languages and sales of more than 10 million copies.

WHY THE WORLD HAS NOT BEEN CURED – YET

Millions of smokers have quit with Allen Carr's Easyway, yet smoking remains the world's No.1 killer disease. How do cigarettes maintain their grip on society, and how can you escape?

At first I thought it would take about five minutes to persuade any reasonably intelligent smoker to quit, merely by explaining two simple facts:

1. The only pleasure or crutch smokers receive when they light up is the perceived relief of the empty, insecure feeling of the body withdrawing from nicotine which non-smokers don't suffer from anyway.

2. Each cigarette, far from relieving the empty feeling, actually causes it, so the perception of a pleasure or crutch is an illusion. It's like putting on tight shoes to get the pleasure or relief of removing them.

I estimated it would take about ten years to cure the world of smoking. Yet here we are, over a quarter of a century later, and there are more smokers on the planet than ever before, an estimated 1.3 billion worldwide.

Smoking is the world's No.1 killer disease, accounting for at least five million deaths every year. This figure is rising fast and the World Health Organization predicts it will double by 2020.

People continue to puff away despite widespread laws against tobacco advertising and bans on smoking in public places. The harder governments make it for the tobacco industry to advertise, the more ingenious the industry gets at conveying its insidious messages.

As anyone who works in marketing will tell you, direct advertising is a relatively expensive, crude and inefficient way of spreading a message. Far better to place your products in everyday

> ●●● **FACT** ●●●●
> Doctors think telling us each cigarette takes over seven minutes off your life will help us quit, but smokers know it's killing them and don't stop.

situations and create the impression that they're part of a desirable lifestyle. If you can place them in the hands of celebrity role models, so much the better.

At the start of the 1980s smoking had almost disappeared from our screens. Surely it's no coincidence that since the bans on advertising and smoking in public places have come into force, smoking in Hollywood movies has risen to the same level as the 1940s and '50s.

On the small screen as well as the big, we've seen an epidemic of programmes with heroes who smoke. It costs a lot of money to make a TV series, and a great deal more to make a movie, and product placement by the tobacco industry helps to pay those bills and enables Big Tobacco to spread its influence in ever more sophisticated ways.

Big Hollywood film-makers are reported to have been paid millions of dollars to feature smoking in their films. Celebrity actors and models are also reported to have been paid huge sums to smoke on screen, on the catwalk and in public. Images of celebrities with cigarettes are plastered across every magazine and newspaper. None of this is accidental.

Actress Corinne Calvet: stars of Hollywood's Golden Era were paid a fortune to smoke on screen

However, the tobacco industry and its tactics aren't the reason I failed to cure the world of smoking within ten years. I first had to convince smokers themselves, as well as the rest of society, that they were not smoking because they chose to, but because they had fallen into a trap.

In fact, the chief ingenuity of the trap is that it can take years to realise you're in it! In my naivety I thought that if there were a magic button smokers could press to wake up the next morning as if they had never lit the first cigarette, all smokers would immediately press it. But I soon learned that many smokers suffer the common misconception that they're in control. If you're one of them, think again!

YOU DO NOT CHOOSE TO SMOKE

If you were in control of your smoking, you wouldn't be reading this book. If you could simply choose whether to smoke or not, you would choose to be a non-smoker.

SUMMARY

- *Nicotine is the addictive poison which hooks you. It's the No.1 killer.*

- *Smokers go on smoking despite all the obvious disadvantages because they're in a trap.*

- *Nicotine addiction is what keeps smokers smoking. It's a disease.*

- *You are not in control of your smoking. The cigarette controls you.*

CHAPTER 2

THE TRAP

IN THIS CHAPTER
• FEAR KEEPS YOU SMOKING • THE NICOTINE TRAP
• THE LITTLE NICOTINE MONSTER IN THE BODY
• THE BIG MONSTER IN THE MIND • ESCAPING THE TRAP

Many long-term prisoners apparently commit crimes on release not because they believe that crime pays, but because it's the only way to get back to the "security" of the prison. This helps us to understand why a smoker with a heavy cough, who clearly gets no pleasure from smoking, continues to smoke. It can be summed up in one word: **FEAR**

To such a smoker, the fear of remaining in the trap is sometimes smaller than the fear of being released. Let me make it absolutely clear: every smoker will feel far happier and more secure when they escape from the nicotine prison.

Why do smokers spend all their lives blocking their minds to the many powerful reasons not to smoke and search for any flimsy excuse to have just one more cigarette?

THE NICOTINE TRAP

There's a constant tug-of-war of fear in the smoker's mind. On one side: "It's killing me, costing me a fortune, filthy, disgusting and controlling my life!" On the other side: "How can I enjoy life without my little pleasure or handle stress without my little crutch? Have I the willpower and strength to go through the awful trauma of trying to quit? Will I ever be completely free from the craving?"

You might have questioned the description of smoking as a disease in the first chapter. Perhaps you interpret this as meaning smoking is the cause of other diseases. That's not what I mean. Smoking itself is a disease; a disease called nicotine addiction. It is now categorised as such by the medical profession.

What's more, nicotine addiction is not just an unfortunate side-effect of being a smoker, it is the ONLY reason people smoke. Smokers are hooked, like the fish on the angler's line.

Why are we so reluctant to face up to the truth about smoking? Why do we ignore the stark warning on every packet we buy? Why are parents so terrified of their children falling into the heroin trap, which kills far fewer people than smoking, yet seem oblivious to the fact that so many of them are themselves in the No.1 killer trap?

Soon after I set up my first clinic in 1983, the disease that terrified everyone was AIDS. We were just learning the terrible truth about it and it was very frightening. In the UK it was predicted that by 1990, 3,000 people would have died. There was a sense that the very existence of the human race was under threat. Yet for many years, over 2,000 UK citizens had been dying every week, year in, year out, from smoking and the figures for the rest of the world painted a similar picture.

As smokers, we console ourselves with the thought that it won't happen to us, or that we'll stop before it gets to that stage. Even so, we still sentence ourselves to a lifetime of bad breath, stained teeth, wheezing, coughing, misery and lethargy. Why does the sheer slavery of it never dawn on us?

Most of our smoking is done without thinking. The only times we are aware of it are when we're coughing and spluttering and wishing we'd never started; or when we're breathing smoke into the face of a non-smoker and feeling stupid and anti-social; or when we're low on cigarettes and panic sets in; or when we're in situations where society won't allow us to smoke and we're feeling deprived and miserable.

What sort of pleasure is it that, when you're doing it, you're either not aware that you're doing it or, if you are aware, wish that you weren't? It's only when you can't do it that it seems so precious.

Perhaps you're thinking it's the tobacco companies, those peddlers of death, who are to blame for your addiction. In reality the tobacco industry is only a part of the problem. Powerful and ingenious as it might be, it's not Big Tobacco that has proved my main obstacle to eradicating smoking.

I underestimated the sheer incompetence, apathy, ignorance, ineptitude and stupidity of the very institutions that you would expect to be my strongest allies, institutions that purport to care, such as the established medical profession and all its so-called experts, ASH, QUIT, the National Institute for Clinical Excellence (NICE), the government, the Civil Service and the media, all of which, far from assisting poor smokers to get free, persist in giving them advice that is almost guaranteed to ensure their slavery for life!

They perpetuate the myths that smoking is a habit, a pleasure, a crutch; that smokers smoke because they choose to; that smokers enjoy smoking; and the greatest myth of all: that it's difficult to stop.

The psychology of nicotine addicts means that hardline measures such as bans and stark health warnings don't stop them. In fact, they only reinforce the myth that it's very hard to quit. Let me make this absolutely clear now:

IT IS EASY TO QUIT SMOKING!

You probably find this difficult to believe if, like me, you've made agonising and ultimately fruitless attempts in the past. You can make the simplest of tasks impossible by going about it the wrong way. With Allen Carr's Easyway, you can enjoy being free from the moment you extinguish your final cigarette.

All the institutions I mentioned will tell you that stopping smoking requires immense willpower. They advocate nicotine products or other substitutes to help you through the pain of withdrawal. By doing so, they are pushing you deeper into the trap. And you won't escape until you understand why:

QUITTING DOES NOT REQUIRE WILLPOWER
WITHDRAWAL CAUSES NO PHYSICAL PAIN

Your addiction to smoking is 1% physical and 99% mental. When you stop, the nicotine leaves your body very quickly and there's no pain.

If you could isolate the physical feeling, it would barely register as a small itch. I call this the Little Nicotine Monster. There is also a Big Monster in your mind. This is the brainwashing that tells you smoking is your crutch, your pleasure and that you can't live without it. When the nicotine level in your body falls, the Little Nicotine Monster triggers a pang around the stomach area which the Big Monster interprets as: "I want a cigarette." This is the nicotine trap – the ingenious way that cigarettes turn smokers into slaves. Each cigarette causes the craving for the next, to fill the emptiness caused by the nicotine leaving your body. And so it goes on, ad infinitum.

ESCAPING THE TRAP

All we have to do is destroy the Big Monster. There is only one way to do that. Not through willpower, not through substitutes. The only way to quit successfully without feeling deprived is to remove the brainwashing that has given birth to the Big Monster in your mind.

The purpose of this book is to show you how you've been lured into the nicotine trap; to remove all the myths and illusions that keep you hooked; to show you how to escape and stay free; and to help you and millions like you *Stop Smoking Now*.

To do that you need to understand and follow ALL the

instructions. You may find some things I say excessively dogmatic. The method depends on you achieving a certain frame of mind, and is the result of over 25 years of experience. Therefore, my FIRST INSTRUCTION is, if I ask you to do something, or not to do something, please follow my instructions – every time.

It's important that you fully understand what you read. Don't assume something is obvious, think everything through. Question your own views and preconceptions. By the time you come to smoke your final cigarette, you will need to understand, without a shadow of doubt, why there is no reason to desire a cigarette ever again in your life.

Finally, as you read this book, don't try to cut down, keep smoking as normal. And don't stop until I ask you to. Don't worry, at the end you'll be stubbing out your final cigarette with a feeling of elation.

....
"I was exhilarated by a new sense of freedom."
....

Celia Hall, Medical Editor, The Independent

SUMMARY

- *The smoker's mind is a tug-of-war of fear.*

- *Meet the Little Nicotine Monster.*

- *There is no physical pain from nicotine withdrawal.*

- *Meet the Big Monster.*

- *The addiction is 99% in the mind.*

- *There is an easy way to quit.*

- *It requires no willpower or substitutes.*

- *Keep smoking as normal until you're ready to break free.*

CHAPTER 3

THE MYTH

IN THIS CHAPTER
• *HOW THE ADDICTION STARTS* • *ALARM BELLS*
• *THAT EMPTY FEELING* • *ONE CIGARETTE LEADS TO ANOTHER*
• *RE-PROGRAMMING YOUR BRAIN* • *THE KEY TO ESCAPE*

THE ENJOYMENT DELUSION

Smokers who insist that they get genuine pleasure from
cigarettes can be very convincing

There are many intelligent, strong-willed, dominant people who only smoke a few cigarettes a day. They assure you they can go days without cigarettes if they have a mind to. Now why do they feel the need to impress that upon you? If they had been explaining to you how much they enjoyed playing golf, would they feel the need to say, "Mind you, I can go days without playing if I want to"?

We are well aware there are powerful reasons not to smoke long before we fall into the nicotine trap, but the trap is so ingenious that practically everyone tries a cigarette eventually. If you ask a youngster why they have taken up smoking, they'll say they enjoy it. But it's obvious they don't. The taste and smell are disgusting and they daren't even inhale in case it induces a coughing fit or makes them sick.

Ask them again a few weeks later and they'll say, "I enjoy the taste and smell." This time, they're not lying. They actually believe it to be true, but what they are really saying is they've got used to the vile taste and smell. After a few more weeks they'll answer the same question by saying, "It relaxes me. It helps me concentrate. It gives me confidence."

So, in this short period, the cigarette has miraculously changed from something that tasted and smelled disgusting into something that not only tastes and smells good, but is also a crutch. There's nothing different about the cigarette; it's just the youngster's perception of it that has changed. But it doesn't last. Ask again a few years later and the answer is likely to be, "It's just a habit I got into."

Why do we no longer say, "Because I enjoy it" or "It gives me confidence" and start saying, "It's just a habit"? Because we sense that it's not giving us whatever pleasure or crutch we once thought it did and we wish we'd never started. The trouble is, when we try to quit by using willpower, we feel deprived and miserable and are unable to stop. Now we begin to realise we're hooked.

Ask the same question years later when you've reached the stage where you can feel each cigarette is killing you, when you lie in bed every night hoping you'll wake up the next morning, either with no desire to smoke or with sufficient willpower to fight the temptation, then you know the only honest reply is: "I'M AN ADDICT!"

Our excuses for smoking keep changing, but the actual reason never does. The real reason we smoke is to try to end that empty, insecure feeling that the first cigarette created. But of course, each cigarette doesn't end that feeling; on the contrary, it prolongs it and guarantees that you suffer it again and again for the rest of your life.

But it doesn't have to be that way. Once we've removed the brainwashing and shattered all the illusions and misconceptions about smoking, you will find it easy to get free. If we had listened to and followed our natural instincts, we would never have got hooked in the first place.

RELY ON YOUR INSTINCTS

As we have adapted for modern life, we have undermined many of the instinctive responses that are vital for our survival. The human body is instilled with certain innate guiding forces, of which the survival instinct is the most powerful. Survival depends on a number of natural responses, such as fear, pain, tiredness – ironically things that we often regard as weaknesses. You may equate fear with cowardice, but without a fear of fire, of heights, of drowning, or of being attacked, we would wander blindly into all sorts of deadly situations.

At Allen Carr's Easyway clinics, smokers often say, "I suffer with my nerves," as if feeling nervous were a disease. But if someone slams the door and you jump out of your seat, that isn't bad nerves, that's good nerves. It's the same instinct that triggers birds to take flight at the slightest sound and escape the cat.

Similarly, tiredness and pain are not evils, they're warning lights. Tiredness is your body telling you that you need to rest; pain is telling you that part of your body is being attacked and you need to respond.

I used to joke that I spent half my life damaging my throat through smoking, and the rest damaging it through talking too much at my clinics. I took to using those anaesthetic sprays or tablets, which helped with the pain. But the sore throat wasn't the problem; that was my body telling me, "Give your voice a rest! If you don't, you're going to create bigger problems." By numbing the pain rather than resting my voice, I was doing the equivalent of covering up the oil warning light on a car dashboard instead of topping up the oil.

....

For years I thought my smoker's cough would eventually kill me. I realise now that it probably saved my life.

....

So much of modern medicine is designed to relieve pain temporarily rather than remove its cause. When we take an anaesthetic we undermine our immune system. By killing the pain, we stop the signals to our brain calling for a fighting force to tackle the root cause. In addition, many of the drugs we take – even those prescribed by doctors – are addictive poisons to which we build up an immunity, so that we end up taking more and more in a vain attempt to escape withdrawal and maintain a state of normality.

In the case of smoking, most of us can remember that our first cigarettes tasted awful. This is a warning from your body: "POISON! DON'T TOUCH!"

Less intelligent creatures would heed that warning, yet the human species has been brainwashed to ignore it. Smokers who are already hooked say, "Keep trying, it's an acquired taste." No, it's not.

IT'S AN ACQUIRED LOSS OF TASTE!

But your body doesn't give up on you. Other alarm bells sound: you begin to cough and feel nauseous – you might actually vomit. Your body does all it can to discourage you from inhaling the poisonous fumes.

If you ignore all the warnings and continue to smoke, you develop a tolerance to the poison. The system is so sophisticated that your body, assuming that you're being forced to continue poisoning yourself, even arranges for you to become oblivious to the foul taste and smell. The same thing happens if you work on a pig farm.

Should you have the sense to cease the systematic poisoning, within just a few days the incredible machine that is your body will begin to eject the accumulated toxins as a matter of course, leaving you as strong as ever. Provided you haven't left it too late!

If this 'incredible machine' works so hard to deter us from smoking, why do we continue to poison ourselves?

HOW INTELLECT LEADS US ASTRAY

Most animals rely on instinct for survival. The human brain works partly on instinct and partly on deduction. It can draw on experiences from the past and, through memory, imagination and experimentation, it can solve new problems. Not only does it draw on its own experiences but, thanks to our ability to communicate and store knowledge, it also draws on experiences and ideas from other generations and cultures. Our intellect has developed to such an extent that it even has the arrogance to question our instinct.

In the past, whenever my logic and my instincts were in conflict, I would back my logic. Today I back my instincts every time. Why? Because I know that my instinctive brain is many times more intelligent than my conscious brain.

FILLING THE VOID

By using our intellect we have dispensed with the need to hunt for food, to gather fuel, to make fire and to avoid many dangers. Shops, power stations, cookers and the law take care of most of that for us. We tend to scorn our instincts in favour of our intellect. The results are impressive: music, art, literature, sport and science – these set us apart from other creatures on earth. But our intellect has also created greater horrors than any purely instinctive creature could devise. The problem begins at birth.

The shock of birth leaves us desperately seeking security.

We reach for it in the form of our mother. Our neediness and vulnerability continue through childhood and we are often cocooned from the harsh realities of life in a world of make-believe.

Before long we discover that Santa Claus and fairies do not exist. We look more critically at our parents, up until now our main towers of strength, and it begins to dawn on us that they are not the unshakeable pillars that we had always imagined; that they have weaknesses, frailties and fears just as we do.

The disillusionment leaves a void in our lives, which we tend to fill with pop stars, film stars, TV celebrities and sports personalities. We create our own fantasies. We make gods of these people and attribute to them qualities far in excess of those that they possess. We try to bask in their reflected glory. Instead of becoming complete, strong, secure and unique individuals in our own right, we become mere vassals, impressionable fans, leaving ourselves wide open to suggestion.

We are forced from the safety of our home, to school and a new set of fears and insecurities. In the face of all this bewilderment and instability, we look for support, a little boost now and then. Our intellect comes up with the solution programmed into us since we were very young. "What do adults do when they need a boost? Have a smoke or a drink."

Is it really surprising that youngsters try a cigarette? After all, you did. Our society programmes future generations to become drug addicts.

Our ability to communicate and absorb information is equalled by our ability to communicate and absorb misinformation.

> Our intelligence may seem to be the flaw in the machine but strictly speaking the flaw is our inability to use it properly. It's equivalent to a factory worker removing the safety guard on a piece of manufacturing equipment to speed up production. The intention is to increase the size of his bonus. The outcome is to shorten the length of his arm.

INTELLECT VERSUS INSTINCT

As intellect wins out over instinct, behavioural patterns are distorted. The key is to distinguish genuine instincts from habitual reactions which are the result of false assumptions and perceptions which have been programmed into our brain.

Our intellect has come to dominate our instincts, triggering unnatural reactions – for example, reaching for an aspirin when you have a headache. You have contaminated your instinctive brain with misinformation and that has become part of the programming. We have no need to smoke before we fall for the nicotine trap, but once trapped, we are repeatedly in situations which we perceive as triggers for cigarettes. Having been convinced that smoking helps us to relax, to concentrate, to relieve boredom and stress and to feel more confident, we now automatically reach for a cigarette in a multitude of circumstances.

So how can we re-jig our brains and get back to that blissful state of never wanting or needing a cigarette? That may sound difficult to you at this stage, even impossible, but I promise you it's not only possible but also extremely easy! All you need to do is use your intellect to replace the misinformed reactions with correctly informed ones. Here's an exercise to show you how easy that is. Look at the image below, let your imagination run wild and see if you can make anything of it.

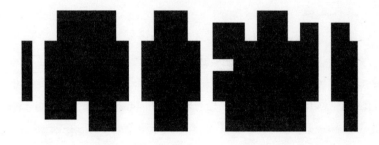

If it just looks like a lot of jumbled shapes, gradually move the book farther away from your eyes and focus on the white gaps rather than the black shapes. You will see the word LIFT stand out.

If you now bring the book closer, it will be just as clear. Why couldn't you see it in the first place? Because your intellectual brain was trying to make sense of the black shapes, instead of the gaps in between them. It was trying to decipher a puzzle printed in black on a white background, when it should have been looking for the reverse. Why? Because experience has taught us that backgrounds are white and information is black, as with the rest of this book.

Now try looking at the puzzle and not seeing LIFT. You can't, can you? Your brain now knows it's there and you can't fool it into believing that it's not. The same thing happens when you see smoking for what it really is: the moment of enlightenment. Like the LIFT diagram, once you've seen the reality, you can't go back to the delusion.

If the brain can be deceived into believing that smoking relaxes us, gives us confidence, helps us to concentrate and relieves stress and boredom, does it matter that it isn't true? Of course it does, because smoking is in reality doing the complete opposite, and worse than that: it's killing you!

It wouldn't be so bad if these delusions actually made smokers happy, but they don't. Smokers remain miserable, irritable, self-despising and frightened. That's the reality. That's why they hate the thought of their children getting hooked. In fact, not only does smoking not make you feel better, it makes you feel much worse.

When you satisfy a genuine instinct or need such as hunger or thirst, you do feel better and that does give you genuine pleasure. Smoking creates an artificial feeling of insecurity and emptiness.

By trying to fill this artificial void, smokers perpetuate it, as the void is caused by the very thing that they believe is relieving it – i.e. the cigarette itself. Addiction creates an emptiness which can only be filled by the removal of the addiction.

A minority of clients who attend Allen Carr's Easyway clinics do not succeed in stopping smoking after their first session. Some then say, "I followed all your instructions. I understood everything you said. I kept telling myself that cigarettes did absolutely nothing for me whatsoever. I kept telling myself that I neither needed nor wanted a cigarette. So why did I fail?"

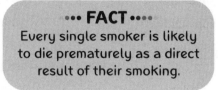

••• **FACT** ••••
Every single smoker is likely to die prematurely as a direct result of their smoking.

The answer lies in the phrase, "I kept telling myself". Why did they need to keep telling themselves that cigarettes did nothing for them and that they neither needed nor wanted one?

I know that heroin will do absolutely nothing for me and that I neither need nor want it, and I don't have to keep telling myself that. The fact that they had to keep telling themselves meant that there was doubt in their minds. They didn't fully believe it. To use the LIFT analogy, they had been told and had understood that the key lay in the white gaps rather than the black shapes, but they hadn't been able to see the word LIFT.

Knowledge is not necessarily enough to beat the nicotine trap. You need to understand the trap and believe the truth that smoking provides no genuine pleasure or crutch. Luckily for the minority of smokers who fail to stop at their first session, back-up sessions are provided free of charge under the clinics' money-back guarantee and the vast majority gain not only the knowledge and understanding but also the belief necessary to become a happy non-smoker.

I will explain why smoking does absolutely nothing for you at all; why you won't miss it; why you'll enjoy life more and be better able to cope with stress; and why it's easy to stop. You may understand what I say. But to ensure success you have to go one step further:

YOU HAVE TO BELIEVE IT

A FAMILIAR STORY

When you smoke your second cigarette you embark on a journey of dishonesty, not just to others but to yourself. You've already broken one vow, the one all youngsters make to themselves, either consciously or subconsciously: "I'll never be stupid enough to get hooked on cigarettes." It's only a matter of time before we break the second vow: "I may accept the occasional one from a friend, but I would never dream of buying them!"

Youngsters think you can't get hooked until you learn to enjoy the taste and smell. As with any drug, the first cigarettes are pushed on them by friends. The youngster has no guilt about accepting these hand-outs because at that stage they haven't asked for them, nor do they really want them. In fact, they sense they're doing their friend a favour by keeping them company smoking.

But the youngster soon reaches the stage where he starts asking the friend for a cigarette and, unsurprisingly, the friend gives him short shrift: "It's time you bought your own." So the youngster meekly obeys. But is it really just to repay the ones that he's borrowed, or is it because that youngster now feels the need for a cigarette, and the only way to get one is to go out and buy some?

We've talked about the void that smoking creates. The reality is that smoking enlarges a void that already exists. From the shock of coming into the world, to the uncertainty of adolescence, we are prone to an empty, insecure feeling, worsened by the pressures of modern life.

Brainwashed by the myth that smoking offers comfort and relaxation, eventually most youngsters light a cigarette. The nicotine leaves the body, creating a bigger void. The second cigarette replaces that nicotine and reduces the void. Sure enough, a secure, satisfying sensation results. The nicotine trap has claimed yet another victim.

As a rule, the more subtle a trap is, the more deadly it is. Take that carnivorous wonder of nature, the pitcher plant. Attracted by the sweet smell of nectar, a fly alights on the upper rim of the plant. It has no fear of the plant. Why should it? It's got wings and can fly off whenever it wants. But why should it even want to? The nectar is delicious. So the fly ventures deeper into the plant, slipping occasionally on the sugary sides, and though it tries to scramble back towards the light, sensing danger in the dark depths, the nectar is too good to resist and the instinct to fly away is suppressed until, too late, it dawns on the fly that it's being eaten by the plant, rather than the other way round.

The nicotine trap is like the pitcher plant, only subtler still.

With the nicotine trap there is no lure. Unlike the nectar that tempted the fly, those first cigarettes taste awful and any fear we might become hooked is brushed aside. "I could never get hooked on this!"

But just as the full horror of its predicament doesn't dawn on the fly until it's past the point of no return, smokers don't realise they're in the nicotine trap until they're well and truly hooked. Indeed, many smokers have lived and died without even realising that they're drug addicts. They believe that they're in control and smoking because they enjoy it. Only when smokers try to escape do they realise they're in a trap.

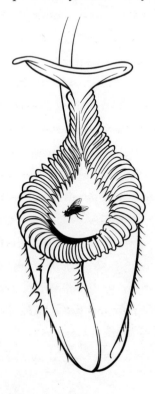

The pitcher plant:
by the time the fly realises it's in a
trap, it's too late to escape. It's never
too late for smokers to escape from
the nicotine trap

IT'S NEVER TOO LATE TO ESCAPE

Some smokers still claim to like the image of being a smoker, the idea that they're cool, like a movie star. Others recognise themselves as pathetic junkies. How can you tell which is delusion and which is reality? As the years go by, most smokers go from liking the image to feeling like a pathetic junkie. Nobody goes the other way.

Once you recognise yourself as an addict, you will begin to see through the delusion. You will no longer be fooled into believing that smoking is a genuine pleasure or crutch and you will find it easy to stop. This is one respect in which the pitcher plant outdoes the nicotine trap. Once the fly realises it's trapped in the pitcher plant, it's too late to escape. Once you realise the nature of the nicotine trap, **ESCAPE IS EASY!**

One of the ingenuities of the nicotine trap is that it makes you your own jailer and this is also its weakness. Easyway gives you the key to your prison. All you have to do is understand how to use it.

To do that you have to reverse the process by which you were imprisoned in the first place. And because the perceptions that enslave you are illusions, once we have removed them, you will already be free. All you have to do is believe the beautiful truth:

THERE IS NO PLEASURE OR CRUTCH IN SMOKING!

Once you understand and accept this, you will not feel deprived in any way. Easier said than done? Not if you approach it in the right way. Consider this: unless you're a heroin addict, the idea of

> ••• **FACT** ••••
> Heroin kills around 1,000 people a year in the UK. Over 110,000 are killed by nicotine.

injecting yourself with heroin probably fills you with horror. So why do you think heroin addicts have this great desire to stick a needle into themselves? Do you envy them? Of course not! On the contrary, you pity them. Why do you see the addiction in such a different way to them? Could it be because their perspective has been grossly distorted by the effects of the drug? Non-smokers see smokers from a completely different perspective too.

TRY TO PERCEIVE YOURSELF AS A NON-SMOKER SEES YOU

I can recall the effort it took to get out of bed each morning when I was a smoker and that depressed, lethargic feeling. I remember the brown fur on my tongue. I remember the suffocating feeling of the first cigarette of the day and the wheezing, coughing and nose-bleeds that followed. I used to boast that I never got colds. "Germs can't survive in my lungs because I smoke so much," I would joke. The truth was, I was so congested from smoking and used to cough up so much phlegm each morning, it was impossible to tell whether I had a cold or not. I remember the brown stain on my upper lip each morning. In my attempts to remove it, I merely succeeded in scrubbing it into a red one. After an all-night poker session a friend once asked me if I was growing a moustache? He was very embarrassed when, on closer inspection, he realised that it was a nicotine stain. Needless to say, there was one person in the room who was even more embarrassed, but the incident didn't stop me smoking.

Whenever I smiled or laughed I would make sure I kept my lips closed, because I was so self-conscious about my nicotine-stained teeth. I hated going to the dentist, not so much because I was afraid of the pain but because I dreaded the inevitable lecture. I remember the haunted looks my wife and children gave me during particularly severe bouts of coughing; the anguish I was causing when they were forced to watch this pathetic creature that was their husband or father, systematically killing himself; to say nothing of the anguish I felt, being aware that I was the cause of their discomfort, yet incapable of doing anything about it.

When my birthday or Christmas came round, I would tell my family not to bother getting me anything. "I've already got everything I need." But I would be thinking, "I spend so much on cigarettes, money that could have been better spent, I don't deserve anything else." I used to feel uncomfortable if another person, even close family, came within three feet of me. I had a phobia about close personal contact, not because I didn't like people but because I was painfully conscious of the way my breath, clothes and body stank of cigarettes. Even as a teenager, I never experienced the pleasure of kissing a woman on the lips without wondering whether she could smell my breath.

My clearest memory of being a smoker is the way I despised myself for being dependent on something that I loathed. With everything else in my life, I felt in control. When it came to cigarettes, I was a slave and I hated the fact that other people knew it. It was humiliating. I hated worrying whether I had enough cigarettes, whether the plane would be delayed on the runway, and whether the next person I met would be a smoker or a non-smoker.

Does any of this ring a bell? Step outside yourself and see yourself as a non-smoker sees you. This will help you to unravel the delusions keeping you in the nicotine trap.

You may be getting impatient now, wondering why we're spending so long talking about the issue rather than getting on with resolving it. Well, rather as if you were a trainee pilot, I don't want you launching into this process before you've got a good understanding of how it works.

Once you've recognised the nature of the trap you've fallen into, Allen Carr's Easyway will provide you with a simple way to get free.

"It is a remarkable fact that Allen Carr, on his own admission a non-professional in behaviour modification, should have succeeded where countless psychologists and psychiatrists holding postgraduate qualifications have failed, in formulating a simple, effective way to stop smoking."

Dr William Green, MB, Chb, FRANZCP, MRCPsych, DPM, Head of Psychiatric Dept, Matilda Hospital, Hong Kong

SUMMARY

- *Our minds and bodies are programmed with survival instincts.*

- *Our intellect sometimes overrides our instincts with false information, creating illusions.*

- *From the day we're born we crave comfort and security.*

- *Brainwashing makes us think smoking provides a pleasure and a crutch which leads us into the nicotine trap.*

- *The second cigarette fills the void created by the first, creating the illusion of pleasure or relief.*

- *We don't know we're in the nicotine trap until we try to escape.*

- *Escape is easy, if you know how.*

CHAPTER 4

FIRST STEPS TO FREEDOM

IN THIS CHAPTER
- *UNDOING A LIFETIME'S BRAINWASHING*
- *SMOKING DOES NOTHING FOR YOU* • *THE FEAR FACTOR*
- *GRASPING THE NETTLE* • *THE RIGHT FRAME OF MIND*

REMOVING THE DESIRE TO SMOKE

*By changing your frame of mind we can remove your desire
to smoke and that's the key to making you a happy
non-smoker for the rest of your life*

So, let's identify what's wrong with your current frame of mind as a smoker, remove that from your way of thinking and let logic and reason undo the brainwashing you've been subjected to ever since you were a child – even before you started smoking.

WHY EX-SMOKERS GET RECAPTURED

A smoker in the nicotine trap is like a person trapped in a man-hole – between us we have the two ingredients necessary to bring about his escape: he contributes a strong desire to leave the trap and I provide him with the tool that will release him. All he has to do is to follow my instructions. However, once out of the hole, we now have a different problem: to ensure that he never falls into it again.

Smokers are notorious for stopping and starting again. So how can we help ex-smokers avoid getting hooked again? The manhole is a physical trap; smoking is a mental trap: an illusion. As we proved with the LIFT diagram in the last chapter, once you see through a confidence trick, you will never fall for it again. Also remember, millions of people have already lived their lives without falling for the nicotine trap in spite of the massive brainwashing to which they have been subjected.

This brings us to the real difference between a smoker and a non-smoker. Obviously, one smokes and the other doesn't, but that's not the whole story. We need to know why. No one forces smokers to light up. They do so themselves. The fact that part of their brain wishes that they didn't, or that they don't understand why they do, doesn't change the situation. The real difference between smokers and non-smokers is that the latter never have the desire to smoke. Allen Carr's Easyway permanently removes your desire to smoke. You will be free.

It's worth remembering that non-smokers have been subjected to the same brainwashing about smoking as smokers and somewhere in their minds they believe that smoking must provide a benefit, but their reasoning has not been affected by nicotine addiction and they're still able to see that there's no sense inflicting the No.1 killer disease on themselves.

The method does not require the power of reason to outweigh temptation, it removes temptation. If the desire to smoke remains, you'll suffer a feeling of deprivation when you stop, will have to use willpower to fight it and will remain at risk of getting hooked again for the rest of your life. We permanently eliminate the desire to smoke so that you do not go through life feeling deprived, vulnerable or having to resist temptation.

Do you think that's impossible? If so, that's only because of the distorted way you see smoking. After all, non-smokers have no desire to smoke – nor did you until you got hooked – and there are millions of ex-smokers who thought they could never get free but have now escaped. The only reason Allen Carr's Easyway has spread all over the world is that it turns miserable smokers into happy non-smokers!

> "His method is absolutely unique, removing the dependence on cigarettes, while you are actually smoking. I'm pleased to say it has worked for many of my friends and my staff."
>
> *Sir Richard Branson*

WHAT SMOKING DOES FOR YOU

Let's pretend that I am going to try to persuade you to take another drug. I'll be honest and warn you that it's very dangerous and in many ways similar to heroin. I make a fortune from selling it and if I can get you hooked as well, I'll make a lot more money. Let me provide you with all the relevant facts.

First, the disadvantages. It's highly addictive and more likely than not you will get hooked immediately and may remain hooked for the rest of your life. It's very expensive: the average addict spends the equivalent of the price of a luxury car in their lifetime. I will provide the first fix free, but from then on I'll make you pay through the nose. Whatever I choose to charge you, and however much you might resent it, you will cough up the money.

It's also a powerful poison, wiping out 5 million people worldwide each year, making it the No.1 killer. As soon as you take it, you become increasingly lethargic, short of breath and less resistant to all sorts of diseases. It causes bad breath, stained teeth, wheezing, coughing, shame and guilt. Worst of all, it imperceptibly destroys your nervous system, your courage, your confidence and your concentration, and makes you despise yourself for being the slave to something you yourself detest. Unfortunately, the more it drags you down, the more dependent you feel on it. Oh, and by the way, it tastes awful.

Now the advantages... What will this drug actually do for you? Absolutely nothing. Not one single thing!

IT WON'T EVEN GIVE YOU A HIGH!

So, are you buying? Do I have another victim – I mean customer? What's

> ••• **FACT** ••••
> The average smoker could buy a house with the money they spend on cigarettes in a lifetime.

that? "Why would anyone cough up a fortune to cause themselves nothing but harm and misery?" Yet, as I'm sure you've guessed, that's exactly what you're doing as a smoker.

> **TERMINAL TERMINOLOGY**
> *The expressions used by members of the medical profession can cause confusion. The word "terminal", for example, induces a feeling of finality and hopelessness. The fact that there are people who have gone on living for twenty years with a "terminal" disease doesn't alter the effect. But the expression "premature death" doesn't induce the same panic. To a smoker, "premature death" doesn't even mean death. It means, "I won't live as long as I would have done, but never mind."*

Why do the facts of the drug that I have just described sound more like heroin to you than nicotine? Because, while we see heroin addiction for the vile, pitiful, deadly condition it is, we've been brainwashed into having a distorted view of smoking. We must rectify this. And to do that, you must understand that the trap you're in as a smoker is the same as that of a heroin addict. You too are descending into a bottomless pit. Unlike the fly in the pitcher plant, you can escape from it, but first it's essential to realise you are in it.

The word "heroin" tends to conjure up a certain picture in our mind: ADDICTION! SLAVERY! POVERTY! MISERY! DEGRADATION! DEATH! The same picture is portrayed by the media and society in general; we're not bombarded by images of happy, laughing heroin addicts. Meanwhile, the laughing, happy smoker is a recurrent image in the PR and marketing of the tobacco companies and the message to the viewer is that the smoker is happy because they're smoking. But they're not. They might well have been miserable if they hadn't been smoking, but that's not the same thing.

Ronald Reagan's father was alcoholic and smoked three packs of cigarettes a day; he died at 60. Reagan himself quit smoking after his brother, a smoker, developed throat cancer

We will remove the illusions from our brain, the part that sees smoking as a social crutch or pleasure so that, as with heroin, we see the real picture. Your frame of mind will be such that whenever you think about smoking, instead of wanting a cigarette and feeling deprived because you can't have one, you'll feel happy that you have no desire to smoke.

TWELVE ANGRY MEN

If you have any doubts about the mental transformation that you are about to make, or if you're sceptical about the power of reason to turn even the most firmly held beliefs on their head, watch the film Twelve Angry Men.

A teenager has been tried for murdering his father. It looks like an open and shut case. He threatened to do it, he was apparently seen doing it, he was apparently heard doing it, he had no plausible alibi and was caught with the murder weapon on him. The film is set in the jury room and focuses on the discussions between the 12 jurors and on the series of ballots that follow. The result of the first ballot is 11 guilty, one not sure. The doubter, played by Henry Fonda, is not able to give any logical reason for his doubts; he even agrees that all the evidence points to guilty. But something just doesn't add up; it's a case where logic conflicts with instinct. Fonda's doubt prompts another juror to point out a slight anomaly in the evidence. It seems an insignificant point, but it leads to further discussion. The detective work is done by the jury and at each ballot the number of guilty votes diminishes until eventually the jurors prove the boy could not possibly have killed his father.

Eleven members entered that jury room convinced the boy was guilty. A murderer! All 12 left certain that he was innocent.

Smokers arrive at our clinics with preconceived ideas about smoking and in various stages of panic. Most are obviously nervous and many are very confused. Their heads are often a jumble of contradictions:

"I'D LOVE TO BE FREE, BUT I ENJOY IT."

"CIGARETTES ARE KILLING ME, BUT WILL I BE ABLE TO COPE WITHOUT THEM?"

"THINK OF THE MONEY I'LL SAVE, BUT WHAT ABOUT THOSE AWFUL WITHDRAWAL PANGS?"

"MY FAMILY WILL BE PLEASED AND I'LL BE SO PROUD, BUT HAVE I GOT THE WILLPOWER?"

"WILL I EVER ENJOY A MEAL OR DRINK AGAIN?"

"IS IT REALLY POSSIBLE EVER TO GET COMPLETELY FREE AND IS THIS THE RIGHT TIME?"

It's not surprising that most smokers are nervous wrecks. But like those jurors in the film, when they leave our clinic, their perspective has completely changed and all their doubts and fears have been removed.

> Smokers suffer the empty insecure feeling of nicotine withdrawal their entire smoking lives. Non-smokers never suffer it and that's one of the great bonuses of being free.

FEAR

In the next chapter we will look at common smoking triggers and remove the illusions that cause them. First we must address the chief ally of drug addiction: FEAR. Fear of being unable to enjoy meals, drinks or social occasions, handle stress or concentrate; fear of having to go through some terrible trauma to get free; and fear of having to resist temptation for the rest of your life. Many smokers who attend our clinics throughout the world say, "I've never tried before for fear of failure." The true reason is their fear of success.

> Ostriches are said to bury their heads in the sand when in a panic, smokers just light another cigarette. Neither activity solves the problem; in fact, they both make it worse.

Just as the fear of failure can help to achieve success, so the fear of success can lead to failure.

The fear of failure is illogical. You are, in effect, fearing a calamity that's already happened: you are a smoker! You might be kidding yourself that you continue to smoke because you enjoy it and are in control, but don't fool yourself into believing that you're deceiving anyone else. Everyone nowadays knows that smokers smoke because they're hooked and have either failed to stop or are too frightened to make the attempt. Leave things as they are and you guarantee that you are one of the failures.

Instead, think about everything you have to gain. Think how proud of you your family, friends and colleagues will be when you succeed. And, more importantly, think how fantastic you will feel yourself.

> The only real problem with the fear of failure is that it can prevent you from making the attempt to quit. Having made the attempt, it can only help you to succeed.

Ironically, the fear of success can be a greater obstacle. It may sound absurd: why would anyone be afraid of success? But when you've been fooled into thinking cigarettes provide a crutch at times of stress and that you can't enjoy life without them, the thought of never having another one is frightening.

Be clear in your mind: the panic feeling, which makes smokers frightened even to make an attempt to quit smoking, is actually CAUSED BY NICOTINE, not relieved by it, and one of the greatest benefits you'll receive when you're free is never to suffer it again.

If I could transport you now into your mind and body just three weeks after stopping, you'd think, "Will I really feel this good?" I don't mean simply health- and energy-wise but also confidence- and courage-wise.

TAKE AWAY THE CIGARETTES AND
THE FEAR GOES TOO

Right now you might find it difficult to imagine life without smoking. Most smokers do until they succeed in quitting. All you need to do is OPEN YOUR MIND.

You didn't need cigarettes before you got addicted to nicotine; there are millions of non-smokers enjoying life to the full and millions of ex-smokers who believed they could never get free are enjoying a quality of life that you have probably forgotten even existed.

Perhaps you've stopped previously for weeks, months or

even years and still missed it. Allen Carr's Easyway is different – TRUST ME.

It's the fear of life without cigarettes that keeps you smoking. I promise you that, if you finish the book and follow all the instructions, you'll be better able to handle stress and you'll enjoy life infinitely more. You'll even enjoy the process of getting free.

SPREADING THE WORD

After I had my moment of revelation, I felt compelled to try to convince every smoker I met how easy it was to stop and how marvellous it was to be a non-smoker. My wife would try to re-strain me, telling me that they didn't want to stop and I was only making myself unpopular. But I kept at it.

When I could no longer treat the huge number of smokers who wanted to attend my first clinic, I felt guilty so I wrote The Easy Way to Stop Smoking *to make the method more widely available. I then gave copies to all the smokers I knew, working on the theory that if a friend of mine had written a book I would read it even if it were the worst book ever written. To my delight, many of them read the book and stopped. But quite a few didn't, and my annoyance increased when I later learned that they hadn't even bothered to read it. I was particularly piqued when I heard that my best friend had actually given his copy away!*

But I soon realised it wasn't lack of loyalty that prevented them from reading my book. In my enthusiasm I had underestimated the dreadful fear that smokers suffer just contemplating stopping.

That book has become one of the best-selling self-help books of all time. However, some readers criticised me for advising smokers to carry on smoking until they completed the book. "Because of that instruction I would only read one line a day," they complained. It didn't occur to them that if I had advised them to smoke their last cigarette before they read the book, that's the last line they would have read!

We are now ready to start removing the fears, doubts and uncertainties which have kept you in the trap. You should be feeling excited. If you feel any doom or gloom, change that frame of mind right now. That is your SECOND INSTRUCTION. [Your first instruction was to follow all the instructions.] You have absolutely nothing to lose. Every smoker dreams of waking up in the morning in the position you'll be in when you finish this book. You're breaking out of a prison. Nothing can stop you from escaping. LET GO OF THE FEAR AND GET FREE!

"It didn't take any willpower. I didn't miss it at all and I thank God every day that I am free."

Ruby Wax

SUMMARY

- *See smoking and smokers as they really are.*

- *Your addiction to nicotine is no different from a junkie's addiction to heroin.*

- *Smoking doesn't fill the void, it creates it.*

- *Follow ALL the instructions.*

- *Open your mind.*

- *The fear of failure is illogical. If you don't try, you've already failed.*

- *The fear of success is caused by the brainwashing.*

- *Remove your fears and you will succeed.*

- *Enjoy the process of quitting.*

CHAPTER 5

THE ILLUSION OF PLEASURE

IN THIS CHAPTER
• *CIGARETTES ARE A DRAG* • *HABIT OR ADDICTION?*
• *FREE YOURSELF FROM FEAR*
• *SMOKERS CAN NEVER WIN*

ENJOYMENT OR ADDICTION?

The greatest illusion of all is that smokers enjoy a cigarette

At Allen Carr's Easyway clinics, smokers usually understand fairly quickly that all you get from a cigarette is temporary relief from nicotine withdrawal and that, since each cigarette is causing the withdrawal, the pleasure or crutch is an illusion. However, sometimes they seem unable to apply this understanding to their own smoking and still think they do enjoy certain cigarettes.

NO SMOKER HAS EVER ENJOYED SMOKING

That is a sweeping statement. Of all the billions of cigarettes, cigars and pipes that have been smoked over generations, did no one enjoy a single one? It seems hardly credible! How could it be possible to create an illusion on such a massive scale? However unlikely it may seem – IT'S TRUE. No one can ever enjoy taking nicotine in any form, whether it be by smoking it, sniffing it, chewing it or absorbing it through the skin. It's essential that you understand this.

> **THE MAGICAL ELIXIR?**
> *If I tried to sell you a potion claiming to increase concentration and alleviate boredom; to aid relaxation and relieve stress; to taste and smell marvellous; to enhance sex appeal, to reduce weight and to provide a social prop, would you believe me? Of course not! You would brand me a charlatan. Yet that's what the tobacco companies and smokers themselves claim about smoking.*

Try asking any smoker what they actually enjoy about smoking when they're halfway through a cigarette. The most common reply will be, "I enjoy the taste." But our first cigarette tasted so awful that we probably thought, "How could I possibly get hooked on this?" So why do we smoke the second and the third?

Some smokers argue that they knew they had to persevere to acquire the taste. The need to acquire the taste for the drug is proof you're already hooked. That's how foul-tasting, addictive poisons work: you get hooked, then acquire the taste – or, more accurately, become immune to it.

Of course, you don't realise that you're already addicted, you think you're still in control.

"I read this book by this guy Allen Carr, and the great thing is while you're reading the book you get to smoke. He tells you when to light up. He's like, 'All right, light one now,' and you're like, 'Absolutely'. And you get to smoke all the way through the book. This guy's brilliant. You get to the last page and he says, 'All right, light your last one,' and you're like, 'I don't know if I want it' – by the time you get to the end you're like, 'I don't know if I want to light it, but, OK, if you say so, Allen.' That was it and you put it out and then you're just done. And I haven't smoked since."

Ashton Kutcher

Many smokers believe they enjoy the smell, although they often can't stand the smell of other smokers' cigarettes and non-smokers find it repulsive. Even if you do enjoy the smell, so what? I enjoy the smell of roses but that doesn't make me want to smoke them!

Once we override our instincts, we build up a tolerance to smoking and associate the taste and smell with the relief of nicotine withdrawal which we perceive as a pleasure. This strengthens the illusion.

Then there's the smoker's perception that on certain occasions cigarettes are particularly special. These special cigarettes tend to be first thing in the morning with a coffee or tea, after a meal, with a drink, during a break, when you get home, after exercise, after sex, etc. They all follow a period of abstinence and the reason they appear special is because the Little Nicotine Monster is demanding its fix and, if you don't feed it, you'll get uptight and miserable and the Big Monster will turn an otherwise pleasant situation into a nightmare as panic sets in.

> ••• **FACT** ••••
>
> The first cigarette in the morning tastes revolting and makes you wheeze and cough. It only seems special because you've gone all night without nicotine, and so feeding the Little Nicotine Monster comes as more of a relief. The dizziness you sometimes feel is not a 'buzz', but the body reacting to the poison.

Smokers think of smoking as a crutch because they believe it relieves stress. However, far from relieving stress, smoking is one of the primary causes. The empty, insecure feeling of the body withdrawing from nicotine feels identical to normal stress. The fact is, while lighting up may appear to relax you, it only does so because it temporarily relieves the stress caused by the withdrawal from the nicotine in the previous cigarette. Non-smokers don't suffer this additional layer of stress in the first place. As a smoker you are therefore permanently more stressed than you will be as a non-smoker.

Nicotine is an addictive poison and our bodies build up an immunity to it, so that even while we smoke, we only partially relieve the empty, insecure feeling of the body withdrawing from nicotine – which I sometimes call the itch – so we start increasing the dose. We inhale deeper and more frequently, reduce the gap between cigarettes and switch to stronger brands.

Below is a graph illustrating a smoker's level of wellbeing as they go through life.

WELLBEING

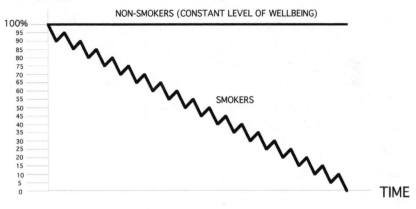

There are genuine highs and lows and stresses and strains in life, but for the purposes of this exercise and for the sake of clarity, we're going to ignore those and focus exclusively on the effect that smoking has on your level of wellbeing over time. We're going to assume that before you get hooked, you're on 100%. Being on a high means having no problems. As a smoker, you're permanently below 100% – i.e. below the level of wellbeing you would have had if you were a non-smoker – because you're constantly withdrawing from nicotine but you're not aware of it because it's so slight and you regard that state as normal. Assume you're ten points below because of the Little Monster and you recover five of those points when you light up. You will receive a little boost, but you're still below the level of a non-smoker. Perhaps you're thinking, "So what? Won't that five-point gain make me feel better, even if it's an illusion?" Would you put on tight shoes just for the relief of removing them? This is what all drug addicts effectively do, but only because they don't understand the trap they're in. As time passes and you go through life as a smoker, you slide further and further down as your wellbeing declines both physically and mentally.

At first it doesn't bother us as we think we can stop whenever we like. But as you go deeper and deeper into the pit, terrible things start to happen. You become lethargic and short of breath. A wheeze and a cough develop. Those cancer scares change from being remote impossibilities to looming larger and larger at the back of your mind. You realise you're not smoking just when you choose to and that cigarettes are now controlling your life. You've got to have them and you sense you're spending your hard-earned money not for a genuine pleasure or crutch but just to be a slave and to risk horrendous diseases. Your wellbeing level is therefore gradually but continuously declining and the "high" you come back to when you light a cigarette is going down in proportion.

The great news is that when you quit you quickly return to the level of wellbeing you would have had all your life if you had never lit that first cigarette. The physical withdrawal from nicotine is easy to deal with and disappears very quickly; within a few weeks the body recovers and, provided you no longer see the cigarette as any sort of pleasure or crutch, you won't feel you're making any sacrifice and **YOU WILL BE FREE**.

We have to suppress our instincts and block our minds in order to carry on smoking. If every time you lit up, you were conscious of the foul taste and smell, the huge amount of money you were going to waste, the slavery and the knowledge that this cigarette might just be the one to trigger cancer, do you think you would be able even to sustain the illusion of enjoyment?

TAKE YOUR HEAD OUT OF THE SAND!

Your next cigarette could easily be the one to trigger cancer in any part of your body, or emphysema, arteriosclerosis, heart disease, chronic asthma, chronic bronchitis, osteoporosis, strokes, diabetes, lung disease, pneumonia, aneurism, or all the other diseases doctors have now linked to smoking. If you smoke it, what will stop you from smoking the one after that and the one after that…?

Some smokers say their enjoyment lies in the ritual: the opening of the packet, the offering to friends, the handling of the cigarettes, the lighting up, the glossy packets, the favourite lighters and ashtrays, etc. It's nonsense. Can you think of any ritual we undertake purely for its own sake? If it's the ritual that's so pleasant, why don't we alter it ever so slightly by not actually lighting the cigarette, thereby still retaining the pleasure of the ritual and at the same time avoiding the nasty parts: the ill health, the filth, the expense, the lethargy, the slavery, the degradation, etc?

Compare it to the ritual of eating. For special meals we dress up and bring out the silver, the best china, the cut glass and the candles. They all enhance the pleasure of the meal, but would you enjoy the ritual if you knew that there would be no meal at the end of it?

Clinging to the illusion that we enjoy the ritual is a smokescreen we devise to justify what is in fact simply a filthy, disgusting, anti-social, expensive and lethal addiction.

THE SMOKER'S COP-OUT

Even after smokers at our clinics accept they are nicotine addicts, some still regard smoking as a habit. It's a handy cop-out. They can avoid the pitfalls of having to explain themselves. It's as if it's no longer their responsibility. It's a habit that's impossible to break, so they can't do anything about it.

It's important for you to understand:

SMOKING IS NOT A HABIT – IT'S AN ADDICTION

The words habit and addiction are often used synonymously. People talk about a "drug habit", but it's essential to be clear about the distinction between the two.

I believe if I'd been taught the difference between habit and addiction, instead of being told how unhealthy, filthy and expensive smoking was, I would never have got hooked.

Why is the difference so important? Because to believe that smoking is a habit, or even partly a habit, involves the assumption that there's some genuine pleasure or crutch in smoking. How else would we have got into the habit? Furthermore, we're seduced into thinking that, provided we don't make a regular habit of it, we can have an occasional cigarette or cigar without getting hooked. Most smokers attending Allen Carr's Easyway clinics require just one session to succeed. However, free back-up is provided for the minority who need it. In these sessions, we ask, "Why did you light a cigarette?" The most common reply is, "I don't know. I suppose it's just a habit." Unless you understand the difference between habit and addiction, you won't fully understand the nature of the trap and you'll remain vulnerable.

....

"If you are one of those folk single-handedly keeping your local tobacconist in business, but want to ditch the demon weed, this is for you."

....

OK! *magazine*

We've been brainwashed into believing that smoking is a habit and that habits are difficult to break. Neither of these beliefs stand up to scrutiny. Smoking is not a habit, it's an addiction and, in any case, if you want to break a habit, it's easy. We get into habits – such as doing certain things at certain times – because it makes our lives run more smoothly, and generally there's no reason to change them. I've been in the habit of brushing my teeth before my morning bath or shower for as long as I can remember. If I wanted to break that habit and brush them afterwards instead, would that be difficult? Of course not! So why do we find it difficult to break a habit which kills us, costs us a fortune, tastes awful, is filthy and disgusting and which we would love to get rid of anyway? After all, no one forces us to do it, it's not an uncontrollable nervous twitch and there's no test to pass. The answer is because:

WITH HABITS, WE ARE IN CONTROL. WITH ADDICTION, THE DRUG CONTROLS YOU

Fortunately, nicotine addiction is also easy to conquer when you understand the trap. Many smokers are under the illusion that they choose to smoke because they enjoy smoking. But if they were to take their head out of the sand and list all the advantages and disadvantages of being a smoker, the conclusion would inevitably be, "You're a fool. Stop doing it!" That's why all smokers and, incidentally, all other drug addicts, instinctively feel stupid.

In fact, they're not stupid. There's a powerful force that more than balances the scales. It's called **ADDICTION**. But what does that word mean to us? All we know is that some unknown force makes us go on doing it against our better judgement. When you try to quit while still believing it's a habit, you think, "I don't understand why I smoke. It's just a habit I've got into and, providing I can survive long enough without a cigarette, time will heal the wound and the craving will eventually go." You're kidding yourself.

You do not smoke out of habit but because you're in the nicotine trap. The trap is so insidious that, even though you may have quit for years, during good times and bad, your brain will remember that cigarettes seemed to help and that can trigger the temptation to try one.

However, if you fully understand Allen Carr's Easyway, you will never even be tempted. I don't mean you will be strong enough to resist the temptation. I mean you won't have the desire to smoke at all.

The force that makes drug addicts continue to destroy themselves and lead lives of misery – the force we call addiction – is **FEAR**! Fear that you won't be able to enjoy or cope with life; fear that you'll have to go through a terrible trauma to quit; and fear that maybe you'll never get free from the craving.

What smokers fail to realise is that the cigarette, far from relieving these fears, causes them. Non-smokers suffer none of these fears. The problem is that it works back to front. It's when you're not smoking that you notice the empty, insecure feeling of the body withdrawing from nicotine. When you light up, it partially relieves it and your brain is fooled into believing that the cigarette is your friend. The more it drags you down, the more you imagine you need your make-believe crutch and the more dependent on the drug you feel.

PRECIOUS POISON

The empty, insecure feeling of the body withdrawing from nicotine feels the same as hunger. One of the ingenious things about hunger is that it involves no physical pain. We can go all day without eating. Our stomachs may be rumbling, but that isn't pain.

Hunger has two other ingenious fail-safe mechanisms. One is that if food goes off, no matter how hungry you might be, it will smell and taste repulsive. This is nature's way of telling us to leave it alone. Unlike smoking, we generally take the hint: have you ever been hungry enough to eat a rotten egg? The second is that, if you go long enough without food, even a rat will become a delicacy. It's all designed to make sure that you survive, almost whether you want to or not.

The similarity between hunger and nicotine withdrawal pangs is one of the reasons we fail to see smoking for what it really is. Because we have eating habits, such as meals at certain times, or a packet of peanuts with a drink, we believe that eating is habitual. Hence, we are led to believe that smoking is habitual. Also, we know that we need and enjoy food and this reinforces the illusion that we need and enjoy cigarettes; why else would we crave them?

But is eating a habit? What would happen if you broke the habit? Exactly! Eating is clearly not a habit, it's an essential process for survival. It only seems habitual because we satisfy our hunger at certain times, with certain types of food and certain rituals.

As an addict you crave poison. The craving for nicotine is a hunger for poison. The addiction creates the illusion of a need. Craving itself, whether for something beneficial or something foul and destructive, is not pleasant. It means you're feeling unsatisfied and deprived. The longer the craving lasts, the more miserable and insecure you become.

Satisfying the hunger for food is a wonderful feeling and a *genuine* pleasure. You can savour each mouthful and satisfy that empty feeling for hours. Trying to end the craving for nicotine provides no pleasure. You have to poison your own body and suffocate yourself. You have to condition your mind to be immune to the foul taste and smell and you derive no genuine satisfaction because the cigarette creates the craving rather than relieves it.

Smokers can never win. When they're smoking they wish they didn't have to. It's only when they can't have one that the cigarette appears so precious. They mope for a pleasure or support that doesn't exist.

Assuming you're a smoker, light a cigarette now, inhale six deep, glorious lungfuls of the cancerous filth and ask yourself what is so precious? What are you actually enjoying about it?

"I stopped with an Allen Carr's Easyway to Stop Smoking Seminar. I wanted to feel free, not a slave to nicotine which does not give you any pleasure."

Gianluca Vialli, ex-international soccer player and coach

```
------------------------ SUMMARY ------------------------

  • No smoker has ever enjoyed smoking.

  • Smoking destroys your quality of life.

  • It's not habit, it's addiction.

  • Addiction creates the illusion of need.

  • The craving for nicotine is a hunger for poison.

  • Far from being relaxing, smoking causes stress.

  • Dispel the illusion of pleasure.

```

CHAPTER 6

YOU DON'T NEED WILLPOWER

IN THIS CHAPTER
- *I DON'T HAVE THE WILLPOWER TO QUIT*
- *HOW FAR WOULD YOU GO FOR CIGARETTES?*
- *IT DOESN'T TAKE WILLPOWER*

UNCLE FRED

Smokers think they're weak-willed and stupid because they haven't quit. But in fact they're as strong-willed and intelligent as the rest of society and successful quitting has nothing to do with willpower

When I and my colleagues around the world do radio phone-ins, we are often plagued by the type we call Uncle Fred. Fred is in his early eighties and tells the story of how he took up smoking during World War Two; how it was his life-saver in the army; and how, when he retired on a small pension, it was the only pleasure that he had left in life. He then describes the awful day when the government increased the tax on a packet of cigarettes by a few pence. No longer was he prepared to be robbed blind. He decided to quit.

Fred proudly explains how, after three months spent climbing the wall, his willpower prevailed and he hasn't smoked since. Bearing in mind that with Allen Carr's Easyway it doesn't take willpower to quit, Fred's story isn't exactly ideal, especially as he always ends with, "Don't tell me it doesn't take willpower. I know for a fact it does."

But is Fred really claiming that, during stressful periods, cigarettes can actually save your life? Does he really mean they were his only pleasure? And was the only reason he stopped because he could no longer afford them? Fred had put up with numerous hikes in the price during his life; why hadn't he got on his high horse before?

Fred's messages are all misguided, and none more so than his assertion that you'll never stop without willpower. If you think that your problem is you lack the willpower to stop, that's because you've not yet understood the nature of the trap you're in.

Ask yourself if you're weak-willed in other ways, or is it purely in relation to smoking? Perhaps you eat and drink too much. We'll see later why that's probably linked to your smoking.

And if you think you must have been weak-willed or stupid to get hooked, think again. It takes a strong-willed person not to be put off by the foul taste and smell of those first cigarettes or by the coughing and nausea which usually follow.

It also takes a strong-willed person to continue smoking in the face of bans, health warnings, anti-social campaigns, etc. And remember, smoking is an ingenious confidence trick which fools highly intelligent people. When you were young, which of your friends first got into smoking? Didn't it tend to be those who were the tough or dominant types? Who are the really heavy smokers you know? Do you think of them as weak-willed or stupid? And what about the idols who sold us the glamorous image in the first place? Weak-willed, stupid people do not tend to become superstars!

> "Friends of mine who had stopped smoking using Allen Carr's Easyway suggested that I read his book. I did. It was such a revelation that instantly I was freed from my addiction. Like those friends of mine, I found it not only easy but unbelievably enjoyable to stay stopped."
>
> *Sir Anthony Hopkins*

We get more smokers from the medical profession – doctors, nurses, etc – at our clinics than from any other walk of life. Is that the vocation of the weak-willed?

If you ran out of cigarettes late at night, how far would you walk for a packet? A mile? Two miles? A smoker would cross the Atlantic for a packet of cigarettes.

National No Smoking Day, billed as "the day when all smokers attempt to quit", is actually the one day in the year when most self-respecting smokers refuse to stop. I was one of them. In fact, many will smoke twice as many, twice as blatantly. That's strong-willed.

Strong-willed people don't like being told what they can or can't do, particularly by people who have no understanding whatsoever of smoking.

PANIC MEASURES

Such is the panic caused by the mere thought of stopping that it can make smokers who are trying to quit actually smoke their next cigarette sooner than they would have done if they hadn't decided to quit. There are smokers who lie in bed every night and vow they will never smoke again, hoping and praying that they will wake the next morning, either with no desire to smoke or with the willpower to resist that desire. For many years I was one of those smokers and, like them, within ten minutes of waking up I would be puffing away.

You only need willpower to stop if you have a conflict of will – a mental tug-of-war.

On one side your rational brain knows you should stop because it's killing you, costing you a fortune and controlling your life. On the other side your addicted brain makes you panic at the thought of being deprived of your pleasure or crutch. We are going to resolve that mental battle by removing one side of the tug-of-war so that all your will is going against the cigarette. Willpower will not make you a happy non-smoker for the rest of your life; removing the need and desire to smoke will.

THE MISERY OF THE WILLPOWER METHOD

Take away a child's sweets and it will go into a tantrum, a self-imposed state of misery. Which child will continue its tantrum longer, the weak-willed or the strong-willed? The strong-willed are more likely to prolong their agony. This is why, ironically, particularly strong-willed smokers can find it harder to quit on the willpower method.

I once survived six months using the willpower method and in the end I was crying like a baby because I had failed yet again. At the time I couldn't understand my mixed emotions. I understand them completely now.

I was in a similar position to a marathon runner who has survived 25 miles of torture. He'll kill himself to finish that last mile. However, if he'd got cramp in the first mile he would probably have given in. I had gone through six months of black depression feeling deprived of cigarettes. Each day I would say to myself, "It would be stupid to give in now, just keep going, eventually the craving must go."

But the feelings of depression and deprivation were like a dripping tap gradually wearing my resistance down, each day getting heavier and heavier. Eventually I was bound to crack and, when I did, I was disappointed with myself because all that misery and depression was wasted. I'd failed yet again. If only I'd had the willpower to last a little longer, perhaps I would have succeeded. That's why I cried.

I realise now that the longer you suffer that deprivation, the more precious the cigarette seems. Even if I'd been stronger-willed, it would have just prolonged the misery. I would still have given in eventually. Trying to quit on the willpower method is terrible and you don't know how long the ordeal will last. While you continue to crave cigarettes, it will last forever.

SUMMARY

- *Smokers are as strong-willed and intelligent as non-smokers.*

- *Smokers will go to any lengths to get cigarettes.*

- *Trying to quit using the willpower method is a terrible ordeal.*

- *As long as you crave cigarettes, the ordeal will never end.*

- *Remove the conflict of will and it's easy to get free.*

CHAPTER 7

THERE'S NOTHING TO GIVE UP

IN THIS CHAPTER
- *HOLIER THAN THOUS AND WHINGERS*
- *THE MILLIONS OF HAPPY NON-SMOKERS*
- *THE JOY OF FREEDOM*

NO REASON TO FEEL DEPRIVED

You're not making a sacrifice as you're not giving up a genuine pleasure or crutch

The willpower method creates the illusion that smoking is hard to kick and nobody does more to spread this illusion than ex-smokers who've quit by the willpower method and spend the rest of their lives having to resist temptation. There are two types: the Holier Than Thous (HTTs) and the Whingers. Both like nothing better than to keep smokers in the trap.

HOLIER THAN THOUS

HTTs are easy to spot: they're the ones who, the minute they've extinguished what they hope will be their final cigarette, put up no smoking signs in their homes, cars and offices. They invite smokers to their homes just so they can forbid them to smoke – and gloat.

HTTs are never slow to remind you that smoking ruins your health and costs you a fortune and that they find it incomprehensible that an intelligent person like you finds it necessary to put those filthy things into your mouth repeatedly and set light to them. They appear to have forgotten that they did exactly the same thing for years. In fact, ex-smokers who've quit on willpower are far more ferocious in their attacks on smoking than people who have never smoked. Here's why: because beneath all the bluster, they've never quite overcome their addiction.

The problem is they still believe they've made a genuine sacrifice. HTTs have a negative effect on smokers who become so preoccupied with resisting the bullying that they lose sight of the real enemy. However, the worst thing is that they reinforce the misconception: "Once a smoker, always a smoker. You might stop smoking but you can never be completely free."

Smokers rightly suspect that HTTs are only so antagonistic because they still crave cigarettes. Their suspicions are confirmed by the Whingers.

WHINGERS

The Whingers are those ex-smokers who, the second you've finished wishing all your friends a Happy New Year and chucked your last cigarette packet into the fire with a wonderful feeling of having finally exorcised an evil spirit from your body, will shake you by the hand, wish you success, tell you how much healthier and wealthier you will be, assure you that you've made the right decision and will never regret it… and then go on about how they quit years ago, but still miss it terribly at times like this.

The effect is devastating. You burn your fingers trying to rescue the packet from the flames and, while everybody else is still busy celebrating, you're sneaking off in search of cigarettes, assuring anyone who notices that what you meant was that you would stop in the morning.

If you've tried to quit by using willpower, you will know the enormous feeling of relief when you finally give in. But can you remember ever thinking, "Great! I'm a smoker again. This cigarette tastes absolutely gorgeous!" On the contrary, the relief is always tempered by a feeling of failure and foreboding, and the first cigarette is always a disappointment, tasting rather like the first-ever cigarette you smoked – disgusting.

I've no doubt that if you've waited years for a cigarette, the relief would be immense, but not the taste or the burning sensation. Don't believe anyone who has recently capitulated after trying to quit if they tell you how great that first cigarette tasted. All drug addicts are liars.

HAPPY NON-SMOKERS

You will shortly be a non-smoker. You may fear never getting completely free from your addiction and becoming an HTT or a

Whinger. Let me reassure you, there's nothing to fear. All around you there are happy non-smokers. Thanks to Allen Carr's Easyway, there are millions more than there might have been. You just tend not to notice them as they don't need to make an issue of it.

It only dawned on me after I had stopped that I never asked ex-smokers whether they still missed cigarettes. This was because, whatever the answer was, I didn't want to hear it. If they did, it would confirm my belief that you could never be completely free, so I was doomed. If they didn't, it meant you could get free and I would have to go through those months, or even years, of tortuous withdrawal pangs again. This is a typical example of the way in which the tug-of-war of fear makes smokers close their minds.

I once knew a bloke called Patrick, a giant of a man, good-natured and, as the name perhaps suggests, an Irishman. We would meet once a year with mutual friends at Goodwood Racecourse. I had just survived a particularly severe bout of coughing and Patrick had that look non-smokers have on such occasions which asks, "What possible pleasure can you be getting?". In an attempt to cover my embarrassment I said, "Patrick, you don't know how lucky you are not to have been a smoker." He said, "What are you talking about? I used to smoke 40 a day!"

I couldn't believe my ears. I'd known him for five years and it had never crossed my mind that he had been a smoker, probably because he was neither an HTT nor a Whinger. I then asked him whether he missed smoking. The reply was a revelation to me: "Miss cigarettes? You've got to be joking!"

Patrick was my first discovery of a happy ex-smoker and he played a major part in starting the process of opening my mind. Having discovered one ex-smoker who didn't miss cigarettes at all, I started asking more of my friends, many of whom I had known for years, and discovered many ex-smokers among those I had always assumed had never smoked. Like Patrick, they were hard to detect because they never missed cigarettes and therefore were neither HTTs nor Whingers. The Patricks of this world don't go around telling everyone how nice it is to be a non-smoker. It's a pity really, because if they did, we would realise that there are millions of ex-smokers who thought they could never get free but have escaped the trap.

Soon you'll be a Patrick and during the first few days after your final cigarette it will help you to remind yourself how nice it is to be free.

SUCCESS STORIES

Go to www.allencarr.com and take a look at the thousands of messages from happy non-smokers from all around the world who've stopped with Allen Carr's Easyway and are now completely free. Soon you'll be able to leave a message there as well.

------------------------- **SUMMARY** -------------------------

• *Quitting smoking is not a sacrifice.*

• *Don't be put off by HTTs or Whingers – they've quit with the wrong method.*

• *You will soon be joining the millions of non-smokers who thought they could never stop.*

• *With Allen Carr's Easyway, you will be completely free.*

CHAPTER 8

THE ADDICTIVE
PERSONALITY

IN THIS CHAPTER
- *THERE'S NO SUCH THING AS AN ADDICTIVE PERSONALITY*
- *YOU DON'T NEED NICOTINE*
- *IT'S THE DRUG THAT ADDICTS YOU*

FUNDAMENTAL MISCONCEPTION

*The "addictive personality" theory gives smokers
an excuse to avoid even trying to quit and is based on
a fundamental misconception*

Many smokers believe it's something in their chemical or genetic make-up that makes it difficult for them to quit. The term "addictive personality" sounds like a recognised condition, but it's really just made up by people who don't understand addiction. It leads to many smokers believing they're attempting the impossible when they try to quit. That feeling is strengthened by their previous, failed attempts and is further reinforced when they learn that alcoholics and heroin addicts also tend to be heavy smokers.

Whingers also tend to support the theory of a "smokaholic" or an "addictive personality". After all, if someone has abstained for years and is still craving cigarettes, they are clearly over the physical effects of withdrawal and, therefore, they must surely have some chemical flaw in their make-up.

No. Don't be conned by studies appearing to link genetic make-up to addiction. Studies can seem to prove a lot of things and many of them are misleading.

Pleading an "addictive personality" is just another cop-out: "It's not my fault. I can't help it! I just happen to have an addictive personality."

It may sound as though I'm accusing such smokers of lying to themselves and their families. I'm not. The delusion is the result of the confusion of contradictory facts, misinformation, anomalies and general ignorance about smoking and addiction that all smokers are subjected to throughout their lives. I'm not belittling smokers, how could I? I sank as low as any smoker alive. There's no such thing as an addictive personality or a confirmed smoker. I promise you, whatever you may think:

YOU ARE COMPLETE WITHOUT NICOTINE

SEEING THE WORLD THROUGH A HAZE
One of the powerful influences that made me feel that I had an addictive personality was that smokers seemed to be a different breed from non-smokers. It's a common tendency to divide the world between black and white, east and west, rich and poor.

To me such distinctions were insignificant. The one that mattered was: are you a smoker or a non-smoker? If the former, it didn't matter whether you were Mother Teresa, Hitler or an eskimo, I could relate to you. Smokers had interesting personalities, whereas non-smokers were boring killjoys. Or was it really that I felt more comfortable in the company of smokers? I could pollute the atmosphere as much as I wanted without feeling guilty. I could cough and splutter as much as I wanted without embarrassment. It only dawned on me after I had quit that most of my friends were non-smokers. Even my wife is a lifelong non-smoker!

THE SYMPTOMS OF POISONING

The addictive personality theory is reinforced by the fact that smokers share certain physical characteristics: the grey complexion, the dull eyes, the lethargy, the dry, wrinkled face. We naturally align ourselves with people who have similar traits to us, an affinity between weaknesses, yet how did we come by these traits? Were we born with them? Of course not. They are all the direct result of smoking, the systematic poisoning of our bodies. Fortunately, shortly after you quit, you recover both physically and mentally.

So, is it the drug that addicts you or is it your addictive personality? In the 1940s over 80% of the UK adult male population was hooked on nicotine; today it's under 25%. Did over 80% of the UK adult male population in the 1940s have addictive personalities? Has that figure now dropped to under 25%? Of course not! Did you need to smoke before you started smoking? Of course not! Will you remain an addict once you've quit? Of course not! Particularly when you get free with Allen Carr's Easyway.

When you smoke your first cigarette, you're hovering on the rim of the pitcher plant. Smoke a second and you step on to the slippery slope, so slight that it's imperceptible. Some people descend into the trap slowly and never realise they're hooked. Others plunge headlong downwards and become chain-smokers almost overnight. The rate at which each individual smoker plunges down the slope is affected by countless different factors, but an addictive personality is not one of them!

THE SLIPPERY SLOPE

Some smokers do appear more addicted than others. Take me: I smoked 60 to 100 a day for 33 years, could hardly perform a single mental or physical act without lighting up and was convinced I could never stop. There were three main reasons why I became a chain-smoker almost overnight: I had a strong pair of lungs that could cope with the poisons; I could afford it; and I could chain-smoke at work. These are three of the main factors that decide our rate of descent down the slippery slope. At the time it never occurred to me that some smokers restricted their intake to ten a day because they physically couldn't cope with more, or because they couldn't afford to smoke more, or because they weren't permitted to smoke at work.

The fact is you didn't become a smoker because you have an addictive personality. If you think you have an addictive personality, it's simply because you started taking an addictive drug. This is the awful effect these drugs have on you. They make you feel you're dependent on them and that there's some weakness in your make-up. That's how nicotine made me feel for 33 years.

Now I have an advantage, I've escaped from that pit and am able to compare the two situations and believe me, there's no contest. One of the greatest gains of escaping is to be free from that little empty, insecure feeling which smokers perceive as a permanent part of their make-up, but which is in fact caused by the cigarette. You also have a great advantage: you have an intelligent mind and the sense to recognise that what I am saying is true.

Do you honestly believe that you were created with a predisposition to nicotine addiction? If that were the case, why is it that it's only in the last few generations, since we learned to mass-produce cigarettes and developed communication techniques that can brainwash the world on a massive scale, that smoking has become such a dominant part of our lives? Do you really think smoking is vital to your happiness or even your survival? If you do, can you explain why you didn't need the drug before you started to take it?

IT'S NOT YOUR PERSONALITY OR YOUR GENETIC MAKE-UP THAT ADDICTS YOU, IT'S THE DRUG

SUMMARY

- *There is no such thing as an addictive personality or a confirmed smoker.*

- *Allen Carr's Easyway works for any smoker.*

- *Smokers identify with each other because of shared weaknesses caused by smoking.*

- *It's the drug that addicts you, not your personality.*

- *You never needed cigarettes before you started smoking.*

- *You'll never need them once you're free.*

CHAPTER 9

DRIVEN TO DISTRACTION

THE LOGIC OF ADDICTION

Do you find it impossible to concentrate without a cigarette? The simple truth is, you're being distracted by your addiction to nicotine

How many times have you heard a smoker say they can't concentrate without a cigarette? During my numerous failed attempts to quit by using willpower, I found I could tolerate the inevitable black moods and irritability. In fact, I used to get a masochistic pleasure from the feeling of martyrdom. But I was convinced that, should I successfully quit, I would lose my ability to concentrate, something that I felt was crucial for my job, and that was my undoing.

I was well-paid to use my brain, and I was under the illusion that my brain couldn't function under pressure without its little crutch. I even thought about asking my boss if he would excuse me from any work that involved real concentration for a month or two, just to give me a chance to quit. In the end, I decided to do it anyway.

The trouble was that there was one aspect of the job that I couldn't avoid, the preparation of the monthly payroll. It only took about ten minutes, and for the month leading up to it I sat at my desk twiddling my thumbs. Every so often I would attempt to do the payroll, but each time my mind would drift away from the task and I would give up. Finally I could no longer put it off. For two hours I sat in a state of blind panic, just gazing at the piece of paper. Eventually I caved in and sneaked out to buy ten cigarettes. When I got back I finished the job in record time! That was all the convincing I needed that I had to have a cigarette to be able to concentrate. However, it was my obsession with cigarettes that was preventing me from concentrating in the first place.

WHAT'S ON A SMOKER'S MIND?

In order to concentrate on something, you first try to remove any distractions. Although as a smoker, you're better able to concentrate once you've removed the distraction of craving a cigarette, you're still less able to concentrate than you would be as a non-smoker for a variety of reasons: non-smokers don't suffer the distraction of craving a cigarette in the first place; you only partially relieve withdrawal pangs even while you smoke; you starve your brain of oxygen; you have to take the cigarette out of the packet, light it, inhale the fumes, exhale them, flick the ash into the ashtray, put it out, empty the ashtray, light another one, and then repeat that process again and again. It's amazing you're able to concentrate on anything else!

PUT TO THE TEST

After three years of studying I had to sit an accountancy exam and was horrified to learn that I couldn't smoke. I'd spent all that time ploughing my way through countless dreary books and, after all that, I was going to fail anyway because nobody had told me that I would have to endure the entire exam without a cigarette. But I don't give up just like that. I decided to find out how long I could last without a cigarette. I got the previous year's exam paper and tried to do it without smoking. My hand was shaking so much I couldn't even write! I thought I would never be able to concentrate without cigarettes.

Yet when it came to the actual exams, the thought of smoking never entered my head. Despite sitting through three of the most highly pressured hours of my life, I didn't crave a cigarette once and passed all the exams. Even though I continued to labour under the illusion for many years, the evidence was blindingly obvious: I was perfectly capable of concentrating without cigarettes.

IT'S ALL IN THE MIND!

Putting smoking aside for a moment, let's look at the nuts and bolts of concentration. The first thing you need to do before you can concentrate on anything is get rid of any distractions. If someone's making a noise, you can ask them to keep quiet or you can move. But say you have a cold and are constantly sniffling. It's a distraction, but what can you do about it? Nothing, so you just put it out of your mind and focus on the job in hand. The point is if there is something that you can do to remove a distraction, you need to do it or else you will become irritated and that creates an additional distraction which can become all-consuming. But if there's nothing you can do about it, it's much easier to ignore it.

When you have a mental block, can you honestly say that the moment you light a cigarette the mental block miraculously disappears? If so, it would mean that you never have a mental block while you're smoking, which is obviously nonsense. So how do you solve the problem of your mental blocks? You do exactly what non-smokers do: you just get on with it!

CIGARETTES AND BOREDOM

Cigarettes do not relieve boredom. If your mind is occupied, you can go for long periods without lighting up and not even notice it. However, when you're bored, you've got nothing to take your mind off the little itch of the Nicotine Monster and so you tend to scratch it. But that doesn't remove the boredom.

Boredom can be removed by focusing the mind on something

interesting, but there's nothing interesting about a cigarette. When you're puffing away, are you really thinking, "This cigarette is fascinating"? There are few more tedious activities than smoking cigarette after cigarette, day in, day out as I did for over 30 years. In fact it's so boring that we're not even aware of smoking most of them. Observe smokers next time you're stuck in traffic. They may be smoking, but they'll clearly be just as bored as the non-smokers. And observe them smoking outside their workplace on the pavements. Do they look stimulated and happy? No, they're bored and miserable.

Smokers tend to avoid doing anything too energetic and feel more jaded the more they smoke. The truth is that smoking causes boredom by making you sluggish, lazy and lethargic and taking away your zest for life.

HOW SMOKING DESTROYS
YOUR CONCENTRATION

When I finally quit for good, I had no problems concentrating, nor did I experience any of the other nasty symptoms of previous attempts. So why do smokers trying to stop on willpower often suffer a lack of concentration? You might put it down to the physical withdrawal from nicotine, but that's so slight that it's almost imperceptible. Smokers' brains have been programmed to believe that any time they get a mental block, there's a simple solution: you light a cigarette. It's this belief that causes the problem. That 10-minute job that I couldn't complete without smoking, there was nothing particularly complicated about it. The reason I couldn't concentrate on it without a cigarette was because **I GENUINELY BELIEVED** that cigarettes helped me to concentrate, and if you believe that then it's impossible to concentrate without them.

If you have a mental block when you're trying not to smoke and you think having a cigarette can resolve it, you will be distracted by that thought and unable to concentrate on the task in hand. If you genuinely believe that smoking helps you overcome mental blocks, you'll find yourself being tempted to try one cigarette, just to see. So you do. Now that your brain isn't being distracted by thinking about whether or not you should smoke, you manage to solve your problem, and so reinforce the illusion that smoking helps concentration.

If you resist the temptation and don't light that cigarette, the doubt will continue to distract you, ensuring that you won't be able to concentrate! The cigarette seems to end up the winner because nicotine addiction is such an ingenious trap. But remember, far from aiding concentration, smoking impairs it and, once you understand the trap, it's easy to quit.

So how do we make sure we steer clear of these triggers that threaten to scupper our attempts to quit, not only for the few days after the final cigarette, but for the rest of our lives?

THE TRIGGERS CEASE TO BE TRIGGERS ONCE YOU UNDERSTAND HOW THEY WORK

BEATING THE BRAINWASHING

There's no point in trying to avoid the triggers. Remember, Allen Carr's Easyway is about changing your frame of mind. Why was it that during my mock exam I couldn't even hold a pen, let alone concentrate, yet during the actual exam I never even thought about cigarettes, despite being convinced that I was completely and utterly dependent on them? It was because there was no uncertainty; I had no choice. I *knew* that I couldn't smoke. It's the same on planes and trains nowadays. Even chain-smokers can abstain for hours if there's no question of being able to smoke. But once they're out of these controlled situations, if someone tells them they can't smoke they go berserk. This illustrates that the problem is not the physical withdrawal but the mental deprivation.

But what happens when there is no one there to force you to stop? Let me make it clear, I didn't find it easy to sit through that exam without a cigarette because I was forced to. What made the difference was that I knew for certain I was not going to smoke. Remove doubt from a smoker's mind and quitting becomes easy.

In the early stages after you put out your final cigarette, if you get a mental block that triggers the thought, "Light a cigarette," all you have to do is remind yourself that smoking benefits you in no way whatsoever; you *know* you've made the correct decision and that no purpose will be served by delving into the subject.

You might find that you can't get your mind off the subject of smoking. No problem; just indulge in a bit of self-satisfaction and self-congratulation that you're free. Then, whether you solve your mental block or not, you'll still feel happy.

SUMMARY

- *Smoking does not assist concentration; it impedes it.*

- *To concentrate, you remove distractions – cigarettes are a distraction.*

- *The belief that you can't concentrate without a cigarette is self-fulfilling.*

- *The triggers cease to be triggers once you understand them.*

- *Smokers can easily go without cigarettes for long periods if necessary.*

CHAPTER 10

GETTING HOOKED

IN THIS CHAPTER
- *OTHER SMOKERS GET YOU HOOKED*
- *CONNED BACK INTO THE TRAP*
- *CLINGING TO THE WRECKAGE – THE LIFE OF A NICOTINE ADDICT*
- *THE LIES SMOKERS TELL THEMSELVES*
- *ROLE MODELS YOU DON'T NEED*

OTHER SMOKERS ARE YOUR WORST ENEMY

Word of mouth is the most powerful advertising tool and, when it comes to cigarettes, the tobacco industry has the biggest sales force on the planet – and it doesn't cost them a penny

What was it that made you take up smoking? Most smokers get hooked because of the influence of their smoking friends and relatives. Some parents think they can get away with the attitude towards their children of "Do as I say, not as I do", but our parents' actions exert an enormous influence on our behaviour. Their lectures on the dangers of sex, drinking and smoking are wasted since they spend most of their lives participating in all three! We should hardly be surprised when our children can't wait for their first taste of forbidden fruit.

NARROW ESCAPE

I've heard countless bizarre stories about the way smokers first got hooked. When I was on TV being interviewed by the journalist Danny Baker, a lifelong non-smoker, I asked him how he had avoided the trap. To my surprise, he said, "When I was a youngster, I fancied this girl at a dance. She smoked so I bought a packet of cigarettes, went over to offer her one and they all fell out on to the floor. My friends laughed and I felt so stupid that I never tried again." Now that's what I call lucky!

If you manage to escape from the pit only to get hooked again, the moment you fall back in is very often linked to a crisis, and the inevitable willingness of a smoker ready to "comfort" you with a cigarette. Car crashes, bereavements, redundancies, break-ups, or even just pressure at work: when these things happen, why do smokers encourage you to breathe poisonous fumes into your lungs?

We need to overcome the negative idea smokers often harbour about what it's like to be a non-smoker. When you're smoking, you convince yourself you're "enjoying a smoke". You may wonder, could you ever sit there thinking,

"I'm enjoying not smoking"? The fact is that you will be able to. I do it every day of my life.

Smokers get other people hooked by propagating the myth that smoking is enjoyable, and they don't stop there. Earlier I described how youngsters get hooked by accepting freebies from friends and then feel obliged to buy cigarettes in return. It's almost worse watching an adult ex-smoker going through the same procedure. They fancy a cigarette and a smoking friend is on hand to supply it, but warns, "You'll get hooked again."

"No way! I'd never buy them," replies the relapsing ex-smoker. Meanwhile the smoker is secretly enjoying the fact their friend needed a cigarette as it makes them feel less stupid about their own addiction.

Eventually, the "pusher" gets fed up supplying the friend with cigarettes, and then comes the dreadful moment when the ex-smoker – who a few days earlier was free of the clutches of nicotine, the same person who swore that they would never buy cigarettes again – has the choice of going without or buying a packet and being humiliated in front of family and friends. The outcome is inevitable. They try to mitigate their feelings of humiliation with the excuse that they only bought the packet to replace the cigarettes they had borrowed, but it's obvious that they're already

BACK IN THE TRAP!

THE SEEDS OF DOUBT

All too often other smokers try to scupper the efforts of those attempting to quit. This was true in the case of a mother who turned up at our Birmingham clinic. She arrived in floods of tears, utterly depressed about being a smoker and terrified of stopping. She also left in tears, but this time they were tears of joy which rapidly spread to the rest of the group. As she departed in a state of euphoria at being a happy non-smoker, she planted a big kiss on my cheek.

That evening she visited her daughter and son-in-law to pass on the good news. Unfortunately, her son-in-law was also trying to quit, but he was using the willpower method and his mother-in-law's obvious delight only heightened his feelings of inadequacy. He muttered darkly, "What are you getting so excited about? It's been less than twenty-four hours since you stopped, nothing to brag about!" His words proved disastrous. She didn't light up there and then in front of her family, but the seeds of doubt had been planted. Her confidence undermined, she went home and started questioning her decision. Luckily, she decided to contact me and learned the lesson to ignore other smokers, especially those who want to pass on their feelings of failure.

It helps to recognise the influence of smokers and, instead of allowing it to undermine you, harness it to a positive end as it can also be a powerful force in helping us to get, and stay, free.

First we must remember:

ALL SMOKERS LIE

They lie not only to themselves but also to others. That's because they have to! It's bad enough being a smoker when we block our mind to the filth, the poison, the wheezing, the coughing, the slavery and the humiliation. If we had to face up to it, the nightmare would become unbearable. We end up believing our own lies, as well those of other smokers.

It takes real courage to admit you've been stupid, particularly when you know that stupidity has cost you your life. Yul Brynner, the great Hollywood actor, had the guts to admit it after he knew his smoking would kill him. The 'Marlboro Man' Wayne McLaren became an active anti-smoking campaigner when he was diagnosed with terminal cancer – good on him! Sadly, three men who appeared as cowboys in Marlboro adverts – McLaren, David McLean and Dick Hammer – all died of lung cancer, earning Marlboro Reds the nickname "cowboy killers". If only smokers would stop trying to justify their stupidity by kidding themselves and others that they get some marvellous pleasure or crutch from smoking, they might save a few potential victims, rather than drag others into the nicotine trap.

CLINGING TO THE WRECKAGE

Remember, at today's prices a 20-a-day smoker spends the equivalent of the price of a luxury car on cigarettes during their lifetime. As you burn that money, you're subjecting yourself to a life of disease, bad breath, stained teeth, wheezing and coughing, lethargy, humiliation and slavery. You'll smoke cigarette after cigarette without even being aware of it. You'll only be conscious of your smoking when you're choking yourself or panicking because you're running out. You will also spend a large part of your life feeling deprived because you're not allowed to smoke. You'll go through life being despised by other people and, worst of all, despising yourself. WHAT DO YOU GET IN RETURN?

THE BIG CON

Kidding ourselves and others that smoking is enjoyable is the greatest service we do for the tobacco industry. Not only do we let their product kill us and pay them handsomely for the privilege, we also do their marketing for them, helping to hook new addicts and dragging ex-smokers back into the pit. They should pay us!

Sometimes our desperate attempts to justify our pathetic addiction sound as though we're claiming smoking is good for us! We've spoken about Uncle Fred. There's also Uncle John. He claims to have smoked 40 a day since the age of 14 and enjoyed every single one of them. Like Fred, he's also about eighty and claims never to have had a day's illness in his life. Every smoker has an Uncle John. We need him to counteract the terrifying statistics society insists on pestering us with. We also cling just as doggedly to his wife, Auntie Jane, who never smoked a cigarette in her life yet died from lung cancer at the age of 50.

Isn't it incredible how otherwise logical, intelligent people happily accept the results of a poll based on a sample of one, yet shun the evidence of statistics based on hundreds of thousands? Such is the warped mind of the drug addict.

Have you heard of FOREST? It stands for the Freedom Organisation for the Right to Enjoy Smoking Tobacco. It was formed by hard-core smokers in an attempt to resist the tremendous pressure our society has been subjecting the poor smoker to in recent years and is now funded by the tobacco industry. This organisation puts a great deal of effort and ingenuity into formulating arguments in favour of smoking. Back in 1992, on National No Smoking Day, I was interviewed on LBC Radio by Michael Parkinson, along with the managing director of FOREST, Chris Tame.

He was an extremely articulate man and started by explaining that the first person ever to attempt to ban smoking was Hitler. It was a cunning opening, implicitly linking the anti-smoking lobby with one of history's most reviled dictators. But his argument, like all those of FOREST, overlooked the following points:

1. Smokers have no freedom anyway. They do not choose to get hooked any more than a fish chooses to get hooked by the angler. Furthermore, they do not choose to remain smokers.

2. Smokers do not enjoy smoking tobacco. They only think they do because they're drug addicts and miserable when they're not allowed to smoke.

> Tobacco has already killed more people on this planet than all the wars of history combined.

When I asked the man from FOREST whether he thought heroin should be made legal, he refused to answer. Where had his support for the freedom of the individual suddenly gone? After all, injecting heroin kills a tiny fraction of those killed by smoking tobacco. What about the rights of non-smokers to breathe fresh air?

While we're on the subject of freedom of choice, ask yourself these questions:

1. How many non-smokers would you say there are in the world who wish they were smokers?
2. How many ex-smokers do you think there are in the world who wish they were still smokers?
3. How many smokers do you know who, if they could now go back to the time when they lit that first cigarette, would still choose to light it?

If you have been honest, you will find that the answers are:

1. None
2. None
3. None.

Nobody wants to be a smoker. Despite all the nonsense about enjoyment, comfort, relaxation and stress relief, just one thing keeps us smoking: FEAR. Fear that we won't be able to enjoy or cope with life; fear that we've got to go through some terrible trauma to quit; and fear that maybe we'll never get completely free from the craving. It doesn't dawn on us that non-smokers don't suffer any of these fears and that the cigarette, far from relieving them, actually causes them. So great are these groundless fears that they outweigh the very real dangers created by smoking.

ROLE MODELS WHO SPELL DANGER

Now we come to a special class of smoker, people who can have an enormous effect, be it conscious or subconscious, on getting and keeping us hooked

Hollywood has played its part by perpetuating the illusion that smoking is glamorous and cool. I have no doubt that this brainwashing was partly responsible for my capture and that of my friends. From Marlene Dietrich to Leonardo DiCaprio, the image of a movie star with cigarette in hand has encouraged countless people to start smoking.

During the 1970s, as the world became more aware of the dangers of smoking, Hollywood made its own attempt to cut down, and the incidence of smoking in films dropped significantly from the days of Greta Garbo, Humphrey Bogart,

James Dean and Audrey Hepburn. However, now Hollywood is hooked again, with the average number of smoking scenes again matching the levels of the 1950s despite the fact that the number of smokers in America has halved over the last fifty years.

There is no doubt that many Hollywood stars, from the past as well as from today, have helped lure countless people into smoking. Many have been

Basic Instinct *(1992) showed Sharon Stone in provocative poses with a cigarette in her hand. Writer/producer Joe Eszterhas, a heavy smoker, developed throat cancer and expressed deep regret that his film had promoted smoking*

paid large sums of money for doing so, though they may not have been aware of the dire consequences for their victims.

And it's not just film stars who act as living advertisements for smoking. Rock stars, TV celebrities, even the characters on reality TV – they all become role models and if they smoke, so too will thousands of their fans.

RUNNING OUT OF EXCUSES

When I had exhausted all the other excuses for continuing to smoke, I took Bertrand Russell as an example. In case you suspect

I'm trying to give the impression that I'm an intellectual, let me make it quite clear, I have never read a single word he's written. I knew only two things about him: he was a genius and he had a cigarette permanently dangling from his lips. He provided me with the excuse I needed: "I don't understand why I smoke, but this man's a genius. There must be a good reason, otherwise he wouldn't smoke."

ELEMENTARY, MY DEAR WATSON

Our heroes often perpetuate the myths about smoking. Take the fictional character Sherlock Holmes, my boyhood hero. His creator Sir Arthur Conan Doyle was a doctor, and I attributed to him an intellect and deductive powers equal to those of Holmes himself. He talks of "a three pipe problem". And I took that as absolute proof that smoking aids concentration.

I wasn't aware of the influence Bogart, Russell, Holmes and numerous other celebrities and heroes had on my perception of smoking. You don't have to be conscious of it, your subconscious brain still concludes: "I can't be that stupid; these other strong-willed, intelligent, successful people are smoking. It must be doing something for them, otherwise they wouldn't do it."

To understand fully, we need to be aware of the influence role models have not only on our children and grandchildren, but on ourselves. It's easy to overlook the fact that smoking is the No.1 killer when a cartoon character like Popeye has a pipe permanently stuck in his mouth. And does that pipe serve any purpose whatsoever, other than to perpetuate the myth that it's normal for smoking to provide an extra crutch for the strong?

Some people argue that the proliferation of drugs, sex and violence on TV doesn't affect the behaviour of viewers, that these programmes merely reflect what's going on in modern society. To believe that is to believe that marketing is utterly ineffective, that advertising is a complete waste of money and that it was sheer coincidence that thousands of teenagers started having "Beatle" haircuts during the 1960s.

The bulk of our knowledge, views and actions are a direct result of information communicated to us from many different sources.

As we realise the people we saw as demi-gods are only human, it also dawns on us that they weren't smoking because it's cool and glamorous, but because they were conned, just as we were, and they wish they didn't smoke, just as we do. Clint Eastwood didn't look cool and tough in his films because he smoked, he looked cool and tough anyway. He lent those qualities to the cigarettes – it was nothing to do with cigarettes and all down to his personal charisma.

"Allen Carr's program… that's real magic!"

David Blaine

SUMMARY

- *We start smoking for stupid reasons.*

- *Cigarettes don't help in a crisis. They make it worse.*

- *Smokers lie to justify themselves.*

- *Smokers perpetuate the myth that smoking is a pleasure and a crutch – don't believe them.*

- *Smokers end up believing their own lies.*

- *Celebrities make smoking seem cool and glamorous, but it isn't.*

- *Nobody wants to be a smoker.*

CHAPTER 11

SUBSTITUTES

IN THIS CHAPTER
- *THE SEARCH FOR A HEALTHY CIGARETTE*
- *REPACKAGING NICOTINE* • *WHY WE SEEK SUBSTITUTES*
- *HOW SUBSTITUTES KEEP US HOOKED*

DEPENDENCY CULTURE

Many smokers try substitutes like nicotine chewing gum or patches, but rather than helping them to get free, they prolong and reinforce the addiction

Vast amounts of money have been poured into attempts to find a harmless alternative to tobacco. By harmless, I mean one that doesn't kill you.

Once upon a time certain tobacco companies even tried to introduce nicotine-free cigarettes. They spent a fortune on research and promotion, then quietly dropped the whole thing. The tobacco industry makes staggering sums from peddling society's No.1 killer; just think what it could get smokers to pay for a cigarette that didn't kill them quite so quickly, and just how many non-smokers and ex-smokers would rush to join them? So, why did it drop the idea?

Well, here's a clue. Ever tried herbal cigarettes? You know, those foul, smelly things that give no satisfaction at all. They might smell awful, but remember, your brand once smelled and tasted revolting to you. However, you persevered with it, whereas smokers never do with herbal cigarettes. The tobacco companies realised that, without nicotine, you could smoke their cleaner substitutes until the cows came home, but you would never suffer the illusion of enjoying them. It dawned on them that nicotine addiction isn't just one of the hazards of smoking, it is the *only reason* people keep smoking.

Nicotine chewing gum tastes awful, but it still feeds your addiction. Persevere with anything containing nicotine, and you'll get hooked.

This is one reason why the tobacco industry is diversifying into smokeless nicotine products. *Snus* from Scandinavia (a teabag-like pouch placed in the mouth) is sold in flavours normally associated with confectionery. Likewise e-cigarettes have been marketed in spearmint, banana, bubblegum and other flavours. The global tobacco players are coming up with their own brands of e-cigarettes at a rapid rate, creating a massive new growth area for their products – ironically supported by the anti-tobacco establishment. Having attempted for decades to use nicotine products to cure addiction to nicotine (in the form of nicotine patches, gum and other products), the same architects of folly now pursue a harm-reduction programme, condemning smokers, one way or another, to a lifetime of nicotine addiction. The idea is that if e-cigarettes are less harmful than smoking, then users will do less harm to themselves by being addicted to them. Of course this suits the nicotine industry, who with incredible sleight of hand are close to having e-cigarettes classed as "medicine". It also suits the tax-raising ambitions of most governments who already earn a fortune from smokers. And it suits many in the anti-tobacco establishment who seem to believe that such a policy will eradicate smoking. The only loser is the poor addict. Make no mistake, the price of e-cigarettes is set to soar as they become more popular.

As if this state of affairs weren't bad enough, the nicotine industry has been given free rein to market e-cigarettes to youngsters as their advertising executives use all their old tricks to make e-cigarettes appear sexy, glamorous, fun, hip, and sophisticated. An increasing number of young smokers now get hooked on nicotine with e-cigarettes.

If you feel like a pathetic junkie now imagine how your kids will feel in 20 years time addicted to e-cigarettes (or whatever the next big nicotine delivery device is) peddled to them by the men in suits.

Most people hate injections. Even those resolute characters who don't quiver at the sight of a needle wouldn't say they actually welcomed injections. But heroin addicts can't wait for that needle to puncture the skin.

Do you really think it's because they're about to obtain a tremendous high? Or is it because they know that the panic and misery they're suffering is about to be relieved – if only for a short while?

Heroin addicts don't really enjoy injecting themselves. It's just the ritual they go through to try to end the awful, panic feeling of craving the drug. Smoking is just the ritual nicotine addicts go through to try to achieve exactly the same thing.

NON-ADDICTS DON'T SUFFER THAT PANIC

Non-smokers can't imagine the panic that makes you light up. There are great similarities between nicotine and heroin addiction. However, there is one key difference: heroin addicts know they only inject themselves to get the heroin, whereas nicotine addicts believe they smoke because they enjoy smoking for its own sake. Smoking is much subtler than heroin addiction.

As long as we go on seeing smoking as pleasurable, we will remain in the nicotine trap, either smoking or searching for substitutes. We think we enjoy it because it appears to relieve the empty, insecure feeling of nicotine withdrawing from the body. Far from relieving that feeling, the first cigarette started it, and every subsequent cigarette has simply made certain that you've suffered it again and again and again. One of the marvellous gains of stopping is to be permanently free from that feeling.

If I had been writing this book 300 years ago, I would have been saying, "Look, there really is no pleasure in sniffing dust up your nose; snuff is just tobacco which contains nicotine – it's just your way of obtaining nicotine and it's the nicotine that's causing your problem."

STUCK ON GUM

We get vast numbers of ex-smokers hooked on nicotine chewing gum attending our clinics; many addicts are still smoking cigarettes as well. We get smokers using nicotine patches who take them off to smoke a cigarette, then stick them back on again. Perhaps this is the shape of things to come. After all, 300 years ago we'd have been sniffing tobacco dust up our noses to get our nicotine fix. Who says we won't be again, particularly if the medical profession continues to back these campaigns to find alternative ways to get nicotine into the body? And why do they keep searching? Are they telling us they don't believe the patches work?

These nicotine products are called "Nicotine Replacement Therapy" (NRT). The term is grossly misleading. They should be called "Nicotine Maintenance Treatment". With NRT, nicotine is not replaced, it's maintained and there's nothing therapeutic about that! More and more you will notice nicotine products which don't even claim to help you quit, but are marketed as a permanent alternative to cigarettes.

This is the sales pitch for Nicogel, a nicotine gel: "Nicogel is designed for the times when the smoker is not allowed to smoke, which is becoming more and more often the case. These days Nicogel is an absolute saviour in-flight, in the workplace, bars, restaurants, cinemas and many other public places."

It hardly takes a genius to realise that giving a drug addict the drug they're addicted to cannot possibly help them to break their addiction. Yet the government and the medical profession, egged on by the pharmaceutical companies who manufacture NRT, have made this practice a cornerstone of their attempts to address the problem and millions of pounds of taxpayers' money is being wasted on lining the pockets of the already mind-bogglingly rich pharmaceutical industry with the effect of keeping nicotine addicts in their prison. This is scandalous.

> Imagine your dinner date slapping a patch on their arm after the dessert, and announcing, "I don't need them, I enjoy them. What could be more relaxing than wearing a nice patch after a meal!"

Actually, what your dinner date with the patches is more likely to tell you is, "They help with the physical withdrawal but not with the psychological side." This is the common refrain from patch-wearers. It doesn't even occur to them that there is no physical problem. The problem is psychological.

One of the arguments the medical profession uses to promote nicotine substitutes is that, even if they don't break your nicotine addiction, at least they don't fill you with all the other harmful poisons associated with smoking.

Well, if you want to remain a nicotine addict for the rest of your life, then maybe they've got a point. But isn't one of your main motivations for reading this book to get free from the slavery of being controlled by smoking? To remain hooked on nicotine in any form for the rest of your life is a horrific prospect. When you ask your doctor for help in quitting, they more often than not prescribe you NRT. This is utterly irresponsible. They're prescribing a powerful poison for a disease that only exists because the victim is already taking that poison, a disease for which the only cure is to stop taking it. Everything is wrong with nicotine addiction, in whatever form it comes and whichever way you look at it.

WARNING: POISON

Nicotine is a powerful poison in its own right. The dictionary definition says, "A poisonous, addictive, colourless, oily liquid which is the chief active constituent of tobacco and insecticides." The A–Z of Medicinal Drugs lists the side-effects: "Nausea, dizziness, headache, influenza-like symptoms, palpitations, indigestion, insomnia and vivid dreams, and muscle aches. Skin patches may cause local reactions. Sprays can cause throat and nasal irritation, nose bleeds, watery eyes, and sensations in the ear. Gums can irritate the throat and cause mouth ulcers and sometimes swelling of the tongue. Inhalators can cause a sore mouth or throat, mouth ulcers, a swollen tongue, cough, running nose, and sinusitis."

PROLONGING THE AGONY

In practice, smokers who try nicotine substitutes virtually always end up smoking again. There's little illusion of pleasure in chewing nicotine gum and there's none in wearing a patch. Eventually, they're forced to face up to what they really are: pathetic nicotine addicts. It's so much easier to revert to the cigarette. At least they can now fool themselves that they're smoking because they enjoy it and go back to huddling together with other pathetic nicotine addicts.

Why do we look for substitutes in the first place? The idea is that you want to kick smoking but don't think you can cope with the withdrawal pangs, so you use a substitute that keeps you supplied with nicotine while you work on whatever else it is that you think is keeping you hooked. Then, when you think your only problem is the nicotine, you gradually reduce the amount you use until, hey presto, you're down to nothing and you don't miss it any more. Simple. But of course it isn't that simple. If it were, NRT would be seen to be working, whereas it has clearly been an abject failure.

Although you know smoking causes serious problems, you also believe cigarettes provide benefits. If only there were a substitute that has all the advantages and none of the disadvantages. Obviously you don't want the deterioration of your physical and mental health, or the cost, slavery, filth or stigma. But you do want the feeling of relaxation you get when you light up.

I have great news for you! That feeling of relaxation is what non-smokers have all the time. The only reason you light up is to try to relieve the empty, insecure feeling of the body withdrawing from nicotine which non-smokers don't suffer from in the first place. In reality, you smoke to try to feel as relaxed as a non-smoker. There is only one way to feel like a non-smoker and that is to become one.

In order to become a happy non-smoker, you need to be crystal clear that you are giving up nothing, only making marvellous, positive gains.

But wait a minute, I hear you cry, what about the severe physical withdrawal? Surely a gradual reduction in nicotine intake is helpful when it comes to dealing with that? NO, IT'S NOT! Some so-called experts believe it's difficult to quit because you have to conquer two powerful forces: the habit and the awful withdrawal pains. If that were so, perhaps it would be sensible to tackle each separately. While you're breaking the habit, keep the body supplied with nicotine. Once you've broken the habit, gradually starve the Little Nicotine Monster by weaning yourself off the drug.

But that is *not* the case. Remember:

SMOKING IS NOT A HABIT, IT'S DRUG ADDICTION

THE PHYSICAL WITHDRAWAL IS ALMOST IMPERCEPTIBLE

To stop smoking successfully, you do have to defeat two enemies, but habit's got nothing to do with it and you won't suffer any pain. One enemy is the Little Nicotine Monster in your body, which is so slight that you don't need a weaning process. The only thing to fear from the Little Monster is that it might trigger the Big Monster in your brain. The Big Monster interprets the withdrawal of the Little Monster as "I need or want a cigarette", and that causes you to feel deprived and miserable if you can't have one. By continuing to feed nicotine to the Little Monster, you prolong the life of both monsters.

Don't turn to any non-nicotine substitutes either, such as sweets, chocolate, peppermints or normal chewing gum. The empty, insecure feeling of the body withdrawing from nicotine feels the same as hunger, but food does not relieve it.

If you use substitutes, you will be moving the problem rather than removing it, displacing it rather than solving it. Do you need a substitute for flu when it goes? Do you search for another disease to take its place? The great evil of all substitutes, whether they contain nicotine or not, is that they perpetuate the illusion that you're making a sacrifice.

"I haven't missed them. I tried going cold turkey. I tried hypnotism over and over again, but this time I feel completely different. My skin feels better. I feel better. I can breathe better. I can't tell you how it works except that it addresses all the psychological reasons why you smoke. I feel really proud of myself and amazed it's been so easy."

Carol Harrison, actress, EastEnders

SUMMARY

- *NRT keeps you hooked.*

- *The tobacco industry has a vested interest in keeping us addicted to nicotine taken in any form.*

- *The pharmaceutical industry, aided by the government and the medical establishment, is now competing with the tobacco industry for the nicotine-addicted market.*

- *All substitutes promote the illusion that we are making a sacrifice by quitting.*

CHAPTER 12

WEIGHT

IN THIS CHAPTER
- *IT'S A MYTH THAT SMOKING KEEPS YOU THIN*
- *WHY HEAVY SMOKERS ARE OFTEN OVERWEIGHT*
- *FILLING THE VOID – SUBSTITUTING FOOD FOR NICOTINE*
- *HOW TO QUIT WITHOUT GAINING WEIGHT*

THIN ARGUMENT

Many smokers using the willpower method put on weight when they quit and assume that smoking was keeping them thin. Here we dispel that myth and reveal how to quit without gaining weight

"I'm not overweight, I'm just six inches shorter than I should be."

That's how I used to make light (pardon the pun) of my ungainly physique. I'm not talking about after I quit, but when I was a chain-smoker. Even though I ate only one meal a day, I was permanently two stone overweight. Contrary to popular myth, smoking did not make me thin. Yet many smokers do put on weight when they quit. I expect you know several people who can vouch for this. I'm one of them. With every attempt, I would put on pounds... with one very notable exception. The last time I stopped smoking I lost two stone within six months of stubbing out my final cigarette.

SMOKING DOES NOT HELP YOU KEEP SLIM

Of all the hundreds of thousands of smokers who have been helped to quit at Allen Carr's Easyway clinics, not a single one has ever told us they made a decision to become a smoker for life. In every case they tried just one cigarette and became trapped. They sometimes claim they started smoking in a misguided attempt to control their weight – but there is no way that's why they continue to smoke. They got addicted like the rest of us.

We talked earlier about the confusion between nicotine withdrawal and hunger. On waking up in the morning, both smokers and non-smokers relieve a series of needs. We relieve our bladders; we relieve our thirst; non-smokers will also relieve their hunger. Smokers, however, are more likely to light a cigarette. The empty feeling caused by nicotine withdrawal is almost indistinguishable from the empty feeling caused by hunger.

This similarity creates confusion between eating and smoking. The problem is, although the empty feeling is the same, food will not relieve the withdrawal from nicotine, and nicotine will not satisfy the hunger for food. The problem is exacerbated as the smoker's body builds up a tolerance to nicotine, so that even when smoking, they don't get complete relief from the withdrawal pangs. Smokers are feeling something like permanent hunger and, therefore, they constantly look for food or cigarettes, or both, to fill the void. The number of cigarettes they can smoke each day is limited by a combination of smoking bans, work, money, the strength of their lungs, etc. When they can't smoke, they will often eat. This is why most heavy smokers, far from being slim as you would expect if smoking actually helped to reduce weight, are often, just as I was, grossly overweight.

"A friend of mine went to see a therapist and stopped easily. Then three more friends went; they experienced no weight gain and no withdrawal symptoms. After seven of my friends had been and stopped smoking easily, I couldn't ignore it any more. The time I spent with Allen Carr was some of the most important and effective since I smoked that first cigarette when I was 14. If it didn't sound so embarrassing I'd tell you it changed my life. It's really easy. It really, really works and you don't put on weight."

Emma Freud, journalist and author

Why do smokers often put on weight when they quit? Because for the first few days after extinguishing the final cigarette, your body continues to experience nicotine withdrawal, and the natural tendency is to search for something else to fill the void.

Remember what we said about substitutes in the last chapter. At first this might be chewing gum or peppermints, but they don't satisfy that empty feeling and that increases your frustration and irritability, while the constant chewing exacerbates your irritability further.

The worst thing is your body and brain are now expecting little rewards, but you're utterly sick of the gum or peppermints and the tendency is to move on to something larger, more substantial and more fattening. Every time you substitute, you remind yourself that what you really want is not the substitute but a cigarette. You take the substitute to try to fill the void, but it fails to do that and instead perpetuates the feeling of deprivation.

You may have heard that you put on weight when you quit because smoking speeds up your metabolism. Why, I wonder, didn't my metabolism slow down when I finally stopped for good, and instead of gaining weight, why did I actually lose two stone? You'll always find an expert coming up with complicated theories when the real solution is staring them in the face. Smokers put on weight when they stop smoking because they start substituting food for nicotine. My book, *Allen Carr's Easyweigh to Lose Weight*, explains how you can be your ideal weight without dieting or feeling deprived.

Smoking tends to make you overweight, not just because it creates a permanent hunger, but also because the resulting lack of energy makes you avoid exercise.

As you feel more and more dependent on the drug and less

and less healthy, you tend to avoid any activity that prevents you from smoking.

A key instruction in Allen Carr's Easyway is not to alter your lifestyle just because you stop smoking. I will explain later. But exercise gets the adrenalin flowing and makes you feel great. It's the best stimulant there is, a real high, and it makes you feel great to be alive! If you're out of condition, start slowly and don't push yourself too hard. There's no need. You've got the rest of your life.

So what about all those smokers who are thin, and all those non-smokers who are overweight? Of course, I'm not suggesting that only smokers have weight problems. As I said, the two are separate issues. But the important point is this: ex-smokers only put on weight because they quit in the wrong way.

The reason I didn't put on weight after I extinguished my final cigarette was that I had experienced the Moment of Revelation. I wasn't feeling deprived or miserable. On the contrary, I felt elated. A dark cloud that had been hanging over my life had suddenly evaporated. I didn't need substitutes. No longer was I a pathetic slave to nicotine.

I WAS FREE!

I can assure you that once you've solved your smoking problems, you'll feel such confidence and wellbeing that you'll be far better equipped to solve other problems, including your weight.

But you must not start picking between meals because, if you do, you may not only put on weight, but you will also fail to get completely free as it's another form of substitution.

Some people believe cigarettes are an appetite suppressant. There are several reasons for this illusion. The first is that when smokers stop on willpower, they feel deprived and tend to substitute by eating or drinking more. That's why they put on weight. With Allen Carr's Easyway, there is no feeling of deprivation and therefore no tendency to substitute, and no weight gain.

The second is that the empty, insecure sensation of nicotine withdrawing from the body feels the same as normal hunger for food, and so we often mistake it for that. We have a cigarette, the feeling goes and we're fooled into believing that smoking relieves hunger when in fact it merely reduces the feeling of nicotine withdrawal at that moment.

Thirdly, do you know what happens when a non-smoker feels a hunger pang and doesn't eat for a few minutes? Their hunger pang disappears. The same thing happens to smokers whether they have a cigarette or not – but when they light up on these occasions they give the credit for the hunger disappearing to the cigarette. They don't realise that they've just experienced the same "disappearing of the hunger pang" as someone who doesn't smoke. Of course, non-smokers can't possibly give smoking the credit for this since they don't smoke. In fact, they scarcely even notice it. If you've controlled what you eat, you've done so in spite of smoking, not because of it.

Have you ever heard of a cigarette brand called "The DIET Cigarette?" Imagine if such a brand existed and on the packet it claimed that, when used as part of a calorie-controlled diet, these cigarettes help you to reduce your weight by suppressing your appetite. Cigarettes are not an appetite suppressant. If they were, the manufacturers would say so on the packet.

SUMMARY

- *If smoking keeps you thin, why are so many heavy smokers overweight?*

- *Nicotine withdrawal feels the same as hunger for food.*

- *The hunger for food is natural; the craving for cigarettes is artificial.*

- *Smokers who quit on willpower tend to substitute food and drink for nicotine.*

- *If you quit with Allen Carr's Easyway, you will have no need for substitutes and you will not put on weight.*

CHAPTER 13

ALL SMOKERS ARE THE SAME

IN THIS CHAPTER
* *WOMEN – ENSLAVED BY LIBERATION*
* *OCCASIONAL SMOKERS*
* *CASUAL SMOKERS* • *CUTTING DOWN*
* *STOPPERS AND STARTERS* • *SECRET SMOKERS*

THE FEMALE

Women's Lib gave women the freedom to do the same as men. Ironically, that included smoking

Women smokers used to be very much in the minority. In many countries, they now outnumber the men. Why has this happened?

Not only have women embraced the habits of men, such as drinking and smoking, but the tobacco industry has spent millions targeting females by perpetuating the belief that cigarettes are sexy, glamorous, sophisticated and aid weight control. Weight gain is a common anxiety for women trying to quit. But, as explained previously, you don't have to worry about weight gain with Allen Carr's Easyway.

I don't think the soaring smoking statistics amongst women are down to their determination to compete with men, though the revolution in gender equality certainly plays a part. It always upsets me to hear a woman describe herself as "only a housewife". ONLY a housewife! If you analyse most jobs you will discover that being a housewife is one of the most stressful occupations one can have.

Feminism has prompted more and more women to return to the workforce, in addition to managing a household and raising children, and it is clear that the woman's role has become more stressful. Gender equality may be a great blessing, but amongst its negative effects is the additional stress it places on women. Given that the main illusion about smoking is that it relieves stress, it shouldn't really be surprising that more women are now smoking.

It's long been known that smoking when pregnant harms the baby, and it's shameful the way society allows young girls to get hooked and then, when they get pregnant, uses emotional blackmail to try to force them to quit at once or be damned for not caring about their unborn child.

Some women are lucky and find that, just as nature alters their eating habits to benefit both mother and unborn child, so they lose the desire to smoke when pregnant. It's another example of the miraculous functioning of the human body.

Other women make a conscious decision to stop, but fail. Even if their baby is born apparently healthy, their failure can leave them with a guilty conscience for the rest of their lives. I dread to think what miseries they suffer if the baby is born with some defect.

Even when an expectant mother does succeed in quitting, it's usually only for the term of the pregnancy. Some women who stopped for the pregnancy tell us that they lit up immediately the cord was cut! You can imagine why. The birth has gone well, all is fine with both mother and child, the fear has gone, the pain and exhaustion are momentarily forgotten, the mother is rocketed from the lowest of lows to the highest of highs: the two extremes that most strongly trigger a smoker's brain to say, "I need a cigarette!" Added to that, the baby no longer shares the same bloodstream and so will not suffer the harmful effects.

Some new mothers survive the immediate impulse and are then caught out at a later date and, regrettably, very few women stop smoking permanently because of pregnancy. If you try to stop for the sake of anyone else, you'll feel you're making a sacrifice and you'll feel deprived. If you stop for the purely selfish reason that you're going to enjoy life infinitely more as a non-smoker, there is no deprivation and you'll be happy to be free.

Many doctors, with the best of intentions, advise pregnant mothers to try to cut down if they feel they can't stop completely. The advice sounds logical but cutting down is more difficult than stopping and, instead of being free from nicotine withdrawal after just a few days, she and her baby are subjected to it for the whole nine months. At the same time the illusion is ingrained in her mind that each cigarette is incredibly precious.

After the birth the mother finds herself in the same position as a dieter who has lost the motivation to go on depriving herself, and embarks on a smoking binge.

We will explain the dangers of cutting down in greater depth later in this chapter. For further information on motherhood and smoking, see my book *The Easy Way for Women to Stop Smoking*.

Whoever you are and whatever your situation I want you to stop smoking because you will enjoy life so much more. Here's a simple adage that I'm sure you agree with in principle, even if it's harder to follow in practice. "If you have a genuine problem and you're able to do something about it, do it! If there's absolutely nothing you can do about it, accept it! Worrying about it won't help in the slightest."

If you're a smoker, you do have a genuine and serious problem. Fortunately, you *are* able to do something about it: **STOP SMOKING!** When you do you might well find, just as I and millions of others have found, that many of your other problems disappear too.

OCCASIONAL SMOKERS

In these youth-obsessed times, when everybody's looking for ways to stave off the effects of ageing while still living life to the full, we find ourselves bombarded with conflicting messages about what we should and shouldn't put into our bodies. When I was a boy it was, "Eat your greens", and "An apple a day keeps the doctor away". Of course, the most popular message has always been:

A LITTLE OF WHAT YOU FANCY DOES
YOU GOOD

It means you can indulge in all those things they say are bad for you, provided you don't do it to excess. This might hold good for certain things in life, but when it comes to smoking it's the worst possible advice. Would you say to someone you care about, "Try a shot of heroin, just a little won't kill you"?

There are two main reasons why ex-smokers get hooked again. One is that they never completely remove the brainwashing, and so there remains a slight, lingering sense of deprivation. The other is that they reach a point where they are so confident that they decide they can have the odd casual cigarette without getting hooked again.

Any smoker who has tried to cut down knows that controlling the amount you smoke will only work for a limited period at best. At our clinics we go to great lengths to explain why casual smoking and cutting down cannot work.

Yet in spite of this knowledge, which is reinforced by their own experience, some smokers still get hooked again because they believe that they can control their smoking. It's the same delusion that leads to smokers getting hooked in the first place. The point is that, even if an ex-smoker thinks he has many powerful reasons to light up, he would not light that cigarette if he knew that he would have to continue smoking for the rest of his life.

BE CLEAR THAT THERE'S NO SUCH THING AS ONE CIGARETTE. THAT WAY YOU WILL NEVER GET HOOKED AGAIN

I've yet to meet a heavy smoker who doesn't envy casual smokers. Casual smokers appear to be in control, enjoying the odd cigarette, but smoking so little as to do themselves no serious harm. It's an illusion.

NO SMOKER IS IN CONTROL

ENJOYMENT DOESN'T ENTER INTO IT

NO SMOKER IS HAPPY THAT THEY SMOKE

THE NEXT CIGARETTE COULD BE THE ONE THAT KILLS YOU

CASUAL SMOKERS

Let's get rid of these illusions once and for all and explode the myth of the happy, casual smoker. True, some youngsters do not get hooked when they try that first cigarette. They're the lucky ones. Some go on to be casual smokers. But don't envy them for the limited amount of smoking they do; after all, you envy them for all the smoking they don't do! What's the point in lighting the first cigarette? If you're lucky you don't get hooked; if you're unlucky you become a smoker. Heads you gain nothing; tails you lose everything!

Perhaps you believe there's an idyllic alternative to being either a non-smoker or a smoker who's hooked for life. A third way: a happy casual smoker. In that case, let me ask you a simple question: why are you not one already? And if you claim to be one, why are you reading this book? Let's establish whether you really want to be a casual smoker.

If I said I could fix it so you could smoke just two cigarettes a day for the rest of your life, would you go for it? Better still, suppose you could control your smoking so you smoked only when you really wanted to. That's a pretty exciting offer, isn't it? But that's what you already do! Has anyone ever forced you to light a cigarette? You've smoked each cigarette because you wanted to even though part of your brain wished that you didn't. So I take it that you'll settle for just the two cigarettes a day. Well, if that's what you want, you can do just that. Who's to stop you? Why didn't you just smoke two a day the whole of your smoking life? Could it be that you wouldn't have been happy smoking just two a day? Of course you wouldn't. Nor is any other smoker.

Sure, there are smokers who can discipline themselves to smoke just two cigarettes a day, but can you really believe that any of them are happy restricting themselves every day, for the whole of their lives?

THE TENDENCY IS TO SMOKE MORE, NOT LESS

There are many factors that restrict the amount you smoke: you may spend time in places where smoking is forbidden, such as at work; you may not be able to afford to smoke more; your body may not be able to cope with any more poisoning; you may be trying to cut down, etc. These factors prevent you from smoking whenever you want to. If these factors were removed, most smokers would become heavy smokers very quickly.

Still envying casual smokers? OK, let's take a closer look at some examples, but bear these two facts in mind: all smokers regret ever having started and all smokers lie to themselves as well as to others.

ALLEN CARR'S CASEBOOK: 1. THE DYING MAN

A man once rang me up late at night and opened the conversation with, "Mr Carr, I want to stop smoking before I die." He was being serious. There was clearly something wrong with his voice. He explained that he had already lost his legs through smoking, now had cancer of the throat, and had been told that he had to stop or he would be dead within a few months. He said he couldn't go "cold turkey", and so was cutting down gradually. He had gone from forty to five roll-ups a day, but couldn't cut down any further. I said, "You are doing the worst possible thing by trying to cut down. Smoke whenever you want to for a few days and then come to see me."

He began to cry over the phone. He explained that it had taken him a year of tremendous willpower and misery to get from forty to five and it had left him a broken man. I agreed to see him the next day.

*Remember, **FEAR** keeps smokers hooked and when they've already crippled themselves, they're even more frightened. Cutting down makes you feel more uptight because you have to wait for a smoke, and it increases the illusion of pleasure by making each cigarette seem more precious. This all serves to increase the panic and the fear, which is one of the great barriers to communication.*

I didn't manage to get through to him in the first session; it was obvious that all he could think about was the fact that he had to stop or it would kill him. But during the second session he managed to open his mind, understand the trap and get free. One of the key points for him was the joy of no longer being controlled by the drug. When he was on forty a day, he was hardly even conscious of smoking them, but on five a day his entire life was dominated by cigarettes.

Prior to seeking my assistance, he had been to see his doctor, whose advice was, "You've got to stop. It's killing you." "I know," he said, "that's why I'm seeking your help." The doctor prescribed a chewing gum, containing precisely the drug he was so desperate to kick.

An exceptional situation? One that you would never allow to happen to you? Stop conning yourself. Millions of smokers reach that stage every year. Not one of them thought it was going to happen to them. You may well join them unless you stop.

Those who knew that man thought he was a happy five-a-day smoker in full control. He wouldn't cry in their company or describe the misery he was going through. Like all smokers, he felt stupid and put on a show to conceal his inadequacy. He lied.

If only all smokers would take their head out of the sand and declare their hatred of smoking, it would be finished in no time. It's only the illusion that everyone else is enjoying it that makes it difficult to stop.

ALLEN CARR'S CASEBOOK: 2. THE GUILTY SOLICITOR
A lady solicitor rang up wanting a private session. I explained that group sessions were just as effective and not nearly as expensive. However, she insisted on an individual session and was happy to pay the fee. You might think, what's so unusual about that? Just this: that lady had been smoking for 12 years, during which she had smoked no more than two cigarettes a day.

Most smokers would think that being able to smoke two cigarettes a day is every smoker's dream. This is part of the myth. We assume casual smokers are in control. This lady's parents had died from lung cancer before she started smoking and she had a great fear of smoking before she got hooked. She vowed never to smoke more than two a day.

That lady was terrified of continuing to smoke in case she too contracted lung cancer. But the less she smoked, the less likelihood there was of illness, and the more precious her little crutch appeared to her. The nicotine trap has many subtleties: the more you consume, the more you want to consume; the less you consume, the more you want to consume! It's like tying someone up so that the slightest movement tightens the rope around their neck.

Do you really believe that lady was a happy casual smoker? The truth is, like the man with throat cancer, she was living a nightmare. For 12 years she craved nicotine but her fear of contracting lung cancer gave her the immense willpower and discipline needed to resist that craving for all but 20 minutes a day. She hated being a smoker. While other smokers envied her seemingly relaxed attitude towards cigarettes, she was constantly battling her addiction.

CUTTING DOWN

Casual smoking and cutting down increase the value we place on each cigarette and decrease our desire to quit. We try cutting down as an alternative to stopping, or as a route to stopping rather than going "cold turkey".

DID YOU HEAR THE ONE ABOUT THE TIME I CUT DOWN?

As well as trying and failing to quit with numerous methods, I also experimented with various ways of cutting down. A popular one is to cut out the routine cigarettes and only smoke on social occasions. In no time at all I found myself in the pub every night just so that I could smoke! It didn't help with my smoking and I was in danger of becoming an alcoholic! Then I had the brilliant idea that, provided I stopped buying myself cigarettes, I would inevitably end up a non-smoker. It wasn't exactly groundbreaking. I'd heard of many smokers who had tried and failed using that method. You may have tried it yourself. The brilliance of my idea was that I had worked out why so many people failed: they felt guilty accepting "freebies" from their friends and that guilt eventually compelled them to buy a pack. This I avoided by warning my acquaintances in advance that, if they offered me cigarettes, I'd accept them without feeling guilty or obliged to reciprocate.

The results exceeded my expectations. Even people who had never previously offered me cigarettes began to do so. It's typical of all drug addiction. When you desperately need a fix, no one will give you one but, once they see you're trying to escape, they keep blowing smoke in your face and sticking cigarettes under your nose. At first it was marvellous. I received a regular supply of free cigarettes! Soon my benefactors realised the devilish cunning of my plan, and one by one they stopped offering. Eventually, I was down to only one source, my secretary. I developed a marked ambivalence towards my supplier typical of a drug addict. Half my brain hated her for supplying the drug. The other half loved her because she was my lifeline. After a few weeks I felt guilty but my ingenious, addicted brain found a solution: she couldn't afford to give me her precious cigarettes, so I'd buy a packet for her. After three months I was buying her three packets of her brand every morning, a brand I didn't particularly like, just so that I could accept them back with a clear conscience and still kid myself I was stopping smoking!

Then I tried the old classic, "I'll restrict myself to ten a day." That seemed to suit me fine as, although I chain-smoked during the day, I could quite happily go all evening without smoking. So I could smoke just one cigarette each hour during the day. I thought I'd have the best of all worlds; I assumed ten a day wouldn't kill me, my finances wouldn't be strained and I could still smoke each hour of every day. I would have a little reward to look forward to. Great!

I soon turned into a permanent clock-watcher. Each minute of my life would laboriously tick away. I was meticulously strict with myself. I would never light that cigarette until the minute hand had reached the "12". Occasionally, I would stand there with the cigarette in my mouth waiting while the second hand reached the vertical before I lit it. What a state to get into!

"I have a very strict rule about smoking. I never smoke more than an average of ten cigarettes a day. Occasionally, I might borrow the odd cigarette from next day's quota, but I never, ever exceed the average of ten a day. The cigarette that I'm now smoking is part of my quota for 4 July, 2046!"

Dave Allen, comedian

We've shown how both casual smoking and cutting down lead to further misery. But what about the casual smoker who seems so cool and relaxed about their smoking that it's hard to believe they're suffering? I'm talking about the one that can go days without smoking and just has a cigarette every now and then. Does that sound like the best of both worlds, to smoke once a week, or even better once a month, or even once a year? I ask these smokers, "What's the point? Do you think you're getting some genuine pleasure or crutch from those occasional cigarettes? If so, why wait so long in between? Who wants to wait a year, or a month, or even a day for a genuine crutch or pleasure?"

It might surprise you to learn that we get plenty of such smokers at our clinics. The heavy smokers in the group clearly envy them and often say so. I ask them, "You're obviously envying this casual smoker who's on five a day. Have you ever tried smoking five a day yourself?" They usually confirm that they have. I then ask, "What was it like?" Invariably they reply, "A nightmare!", or words to that effect. I then ask the casual smoker whether they feel in control of their smoking. They can't even pretend to be in control since they're at a stop-smoking clinic, so instead they're honest and describe what a nightmare it is to be a casual smoker. Then the heavy smokers begin to realise that the casual smoker is going through a similar hell to them, is just as fed up with smoking and just as desperate to stop.

Smokers who go for weeks without a cigarette don't even suffer the illusion of getting a pleasure or crutch from smoking, they just go through the motions to be part of the company. Remember, we all started off like that, convinced we'd never get hooked. They're like the fly hovering round the rim of the pitcher plant and they often turn into heavy smokers.

You might think it sounds nice only to want a cigarette every now and then; but wouldn't it be ideal never to want one at all?

....

My mother-in-law only smoked on social occasions until the age of 60, when she bought a pub. That was before the ban on smoking in public places. Within months she was on 60 a day and died at 65.

....

Casual smokers, like all smokers who try to restrict their smoking, are creating a number of serious problems for themselves:

1. They keep themselves physically addicted to nicotine. This keeps their brains craving cigarettes.

2. They wish their lives away waiting for the next fix.

3. Instead of smoking whenever they feel like it and partially relieving their craving most of the time, they force themselves to suffer additional withdrawal pangs and are always restless.

4. They reinforce the illusion that smoking is enjoyable.

When you chain-smoke, you lose the illusion of enjoyment. Even the lighting up becomes automatic. You will find that these so-called special cigarettes, the ones that you feel you enjoy most, are always after a period of abstinence: the one after a meal, after work, after sex, after exercise, after shopping or the first one of the day.

This is because there's no genuine pleasure or crutch whatsoever in smoking. Cigarettes are filthy, disgusting and poisonous. All that smokers enjoy is the end of the aggravation of the craving.

Cutting down increases the illusion of pleasure because the

longer you've been craving a cigarette, the more marvellous it appears when you relieve that craving. It's like the craving for food: hunger; or for liquid: thirst. You might want to stop me here. "Increases the illusion of pleasure," did you say? "What's so bad about that?" This: it's not pleasure at all, but the ending of the constant aggravation of craving. The only way to increase the illusion of pleasure is to increase the aggravation. No smoker, including casual smokers, enjoys being a smoker. You should also remember that being a casual smoker is rarely sustainable. The addiction makes you want to scratch the itch not suffer it and the tendency is to smoke more and more.

Casual smoking is a terrible form of slavery as you're excercising willpower and discipline to limit your intake and are constantly thinking about whether or not you will allow yourself to smoke. You also labour under the delusion that you can control your addiction.

MANY CASUAL SMOKERS DON'T REALISE THEY'RE IN A TRAP. UNTIL THEY DO, ESCAPE IS IMPOSSIBLE

The tendency of the nicotine addict is to chain-smoke since their body is constantly withdrawing from nicotine. If you're a casual smoker or are trying to cut down, you may try to resist the urge. Get it clear in your mind: you will never be able to control your intake.

Most smokers know from experience that cutting down is a mug's game. You invariably end up smoking as many as before, if not more.

However, fortunately it's easy to escape from the trap completely, so there's no need to resort to half measures. No one is dependent on nicotine and, once you understand the trap fully, it takes no willpower to stop. Even if you did possess the massive willpower required to limit your intake for the rest of your life, would you really want to?

RELIEF NOT PLEASURE

I often liken the so-called pleasure you get from smoking to wearing tight shoes just for the pleasure of taking them off. Who do you think suffers most: someone who can remove his tight shoes every half an hour, or someone who has to keep them on all day? Unlike casual smokers, regular and heavy smokers are at least partially relieving their withdrawal pangs at regular intervals.

STOPPERS AND STARTERS

Heavy smokers think casual smokers have the best of all worlds. But the truth is that in many ways they have the worst: they can neither smoke whenever they want to, nor do they have the marvellous joy of being free.

The same is true of stoppers and starters, who are also often envied by other smokers. They're not strictly casual smokers, but tend to be regarded in the same light. In fact, quite often they're very heavy smokers.

Stoppers and starters tend not to be perceived as poor fools who repeatedly fall back into the same manhole, but as lucky people who possess the enviable ability to stop and start whenever they choose. Of course, such smokers don't like to appear stupid any more than the rest of us, so they encourage the misconception. And of course, it's a lie.

Look at the situation logically. If these smokers truly enjoy being smokers, why do they keep stopping? For the same reason that any other smoker does: they don't enjoy being smokers. Having become non-smokers, why do they change their minds and decide to become smokers again? There can be only one answer to that: they don't enjoy being non-smokers.

What tragic people! Neither happy as smokers nor happy as non-smokers: the worst of all worlds. When they're smokers, they envy non-smokers. They go through the trauma of stopping using the willpower method, but never become happy non-smokers, so they start smoking again. Once hooked again, they remember why they stopped in the first place. They're always miserable.

Remember, to be a happy non-smoker for the rest of your life, you need to achieve the right frame of mind. If you believe you're making a sacrifice, you might never smoke again, but you'll feel deprived. If you regard just one puff on a cigarette as a crutch or pleasure, you'll remain vulnerable for the rest of your life. If you want one cigarette, what will prevent you from wanting another and another and another?

You may think, "If Allen Carr's Easyway makes it easy to quit, what possible danger can there be in smoking the occasional cigarette? Even if I do get hooked again, I can use the method to quit again." If you have a need or desire to have just one puff, then you haven't understood Allen Carr's Easyway.

The whole object of this exercise is to remove your desire to take even a single puff because, if you want just one, you'll want a million. Even if you don't actually have that puff but merely desire it, you will not be a happy non-smoker. You will be a miserable ex-smoker! Eventually, when your willpower runs out, you will cease to be a miserable ex-smoker and become an even more miserable smoker!

This brings us to the most miserable smokers of all.

SECRET SMOKERS

There are many deeply upsetting aspects to smoking. Which is the worst? Watching smokers in the advanced stages of emphysema and finding yourself subconsciously trying to breathe for them rates very high. Listening to a smoker who has just had a leg removed and is trying to convince you it had absolutely nothing to do with smoking is particularly disturbing. Then there are the smokers who have just discovered that they have contracted lung cancer and are trying to convince you, and themselves, that it was all worth it and that they enjoyed every precious cigarette.

However, the most pathetic of all is the secret smoker. They promise their loved ones that they'll quit but don't and then start lying! To break a solemn promise to someone you love is bad enough, but then to compound that by lying in order to cover up your inadequacy is the ultimate humiliation.

If you smoke openly, you can at least claim that you smoke because you choose to. As a secret smoker, you have to admit to yourself that you're a pathetic slave to nicotine. Secret smokers go through life despising themselves. I learned the importance of honesty early in life and yet I still became a secret smoker. I still lied to the people who loved and trusted me. And most pathetic of all, I actually convinced myself that they believed my lies, that they couldn't see the yellow stains on my fingers, lips and teeth, or smell my bad breath or the stale smoke in my hair and on my clothes. Deep down, I knew I wasn't fooling anyone except myself. Smokers lie not because they are dishonest by nature, but because that's what the addiction does to you.

NO HIDING PLACE

The stories we hear at our clinics about secret smoking are often amusing. One couple who attended had previously made a pact to quit. They were very determined. They threw out all the ashtrays and redecorated the house. That attempt failed and they eventually attended one of our clinics where the husband admitted to his wife that he'd been smoking secretly out of the kitchen window all along. His wife replied, "Oh, I know that, because I was secretly smoking out of the upstairs bedroom window looking down at you!"

These stories can also be tragic. There was a mother who stopped smoking because of pressure from her seven-year-old daughter: "Mummy, I don't want you to die." She had tried the willpower method and, as usual, after a few days had fallen for the compromise of just having one as a little reward in the evening. One evening her child wouldn't go to sleep. The mother said, "I was getting annoyed with her because I was dying for a cigarette. Eventually she dropped off. I rushed down to the kitchen. No sooner had I lit up than I heard a little voice behind me, 'You're not smoking, are you, Mummy?'" When I was a boy your parents would clip you round the ear if they caught you smoking; now it's the children who tell their parents off.

Imagine the embarrassment of one of my clients who, visiting his non-smoking mother-in-law in Canada, nipped out for a secret smoke in weather 20 degrees below zero, with the excuse that he needed a breath of fresh air. He returned in a state of panic. He smoked those awful little cigars that have their own plastic holder. The plastic had frozen to his lip and he still had it in his mouth when his mother-in-law opened the door to him. Such is the infinite pleasure of being a smoker!

Although as a secret smoker you lie to others, and to yourself, beneath the deceit you're acutely aware of the painful truth: you're a slave to nicotine, a miserable, pathetic drug addict.

All the various types of smoker that we've discussed in this chapter wish they'd never started. Don't envy them. Regardless of which category they fall into, every smoker would love to wake in the morning in the position you will be in when you finish this book – **FREE**.

SUMMARY

- *Women are not a special case.*

- *The tendency is to smoke more and more.*

- *Casual smokers are constantly on edge.*

- *Cutting down doesn't work.*

- *Stoppers and starters are never happy.*

- *Secret smokers are the most miserable of all.*

- *All smokers wish they were free.*

CHAPTER 14

BURNING QUESTIONS

IN THIS CHAPTER

- *HOW WILL I KNOW WHEN I'VE SMOKED MY FINAL CIGARETTE?*
- *WHEN DO I BECOME A NON-SMOKER?*
- *WILL I EVER BE COMPLETELY FREE?*
- *CAN I ENJOY LIFE WITHOUT CIGARETTES?*
- *WHAT DO I DO IN A CRISIS?*
- *ADDICTION OR DEPENDENCE?*

THE FEAR FACTOR

Smokers are brainwashed into fearing they will never be able
to enjoy life without cigarettes

Smokers are terrified that they have to go through some terrible trauma to quit and that they may never be able to enjoy or cope with life without smoking. This leads to putting off what they think of as the evil day: "Yes, I'll stop, but not today."

All our life we are led to believe that smoking is enjoyable and that it's incredibly hard to kick. With these myths ingrained in our mind, we find it difficult to believe that stopping can be easy.

At our clinics, we ask, "How will you know when you're a non-smoker?" We get a variety of answers:

"When I can go out drinking with my friends or enjoy a meal without wanting a cigarette."

"When I've managed to go a whole day without a cigarette."

"When I feel like a non-smoker."

In all these cases the smoker assumes that they will start off feeling deprived and has no idea how long they will have to wait for that feeling to go.

THE FINAL CIGARETTE

You become a non-smoker when you extinguish your final cigarette. How do you know it's your final cigarette? When you pass your driving test, you experience a wonderful boost. Even though you're no better at driving than before, you now know for certain that you can drive legally. To be free, it is not enough to try, or hope, that you will never smoke another cigarette. You must be certain. If you're not, you'll subject yourself to a lifetime of torture. Imagine suspecting you might have a terminal disease. You go for tests and have to wait a week for the result. If you had to wait a month, or a year, it would be even worse. Now imagine having to wait the rest of your life for that result. That's what it's like for ex-smokers who are not certain they've kicked it. They wait for the doubt to go, but it never does. They spend the rest of their lives waiting for something that will never happen.

This is why smokers who use the willpower method are so miserable. They go through the rest of their lives waiting for nothing to happen. The illusion that, once hooked, you can never

*get completely free – or "Once a smoker, always a smoker" – is
what makes smokers believe they have addictive personalities.*

Why do we go on smoking despite knowing that non-smokers are much better off than we are and that we were perfectly able to enjoy life and cope with stress before we began smoking? Millions of smokers have succeeded in getting free and yet we still doubt whether it's possible for us.

BELIEVING IS SUCCEEDING

Get it clearly into your mind: you won't miss cigarettes and you'll enjoy life more and be better equipped to cope with stress when you're free.

REPLACE ILLUSIONS WITH UNDERSTANDING

You may think that you already understand everything. If so, don't jump the gun. You may still be uncertain. If so, don't worry – all will become clear. Take the time and care to read right to the end of this book.

There's nothing unusual or stupid about believing that stopping smoking is one of the hardest things to do. Society subjects us to this brainwashing and smokers appear to confirm it by using the willpower method. Indeed, we seem to have proved it to ourselves from our previous failed attempts. We don't just think it's difficult to stop, we've also learned it. That panic feeling we get when we run out of cigarettes might well be illogical, but it's also very real, and so is the irritability and misery we suffer when we attempt to stop with the willpower method.

When we're forced to think about it, we readily accept that smoking is illogical. Although we don't understand why we seem to be so dependent on cigarettes, our feeling of panic and fear when deprived of them can be explained. It's our brainwashed mind telling us that only a cigarette will relieve the unsettling, empty feeling we experience as nicotine withdraws from our body. Once you understand beyond all doubt that the cigarette, far from relieving the empty feeling, causes it, you have already removed the cause of the panic. If you have any doubts about this point, read Chapter 1 again.

The willpower method is based on fighting through the panic, and at first, while willpower is at its strongest, it often works. But as your willpower ebbs away and your resolve weakens, so the little voice saying, "I want a cigarette," gets louder and louder. You now find yourself in an impossible situation. You are still determined to be a non-smoker, but part of your brain is urging you to light a cigarette.

We see smoker's schizophrenia in black and white at our clinics. On the questionnaires, some smokers write, "I enjoy being a smoker, but I hate smoking." Others write, "I enjoy smoking, but I hate being a smoker." Imagine an angler saying, "I enjoy being an angler, but I hate fishing"!

Such is the confusion surrounding smoking that smokers honestly think smoking and being a smoker are two different things. Get it clear in your mind: if you smoke, you are a smoker! There is only one essential quality to being a non-smoker: not to smoke – ever!

Is it really surprising that we get so confused, irritable and downright miserable on the willpower method? It would be a miracle if we didn't.

GOOD TIMES

Smokers believe cigarettes provide them with a pleasure and a crutch. In fact, these illusions are simply two sides of the same coin. Let's start with the pleasure. There are a number of "special" cigarettes that smokers fear they'll miss. The most common is the one after a meal. The case of one of our clients summed up the whole thing. He was intelligent, attentive and genuinely committed to quitting. The only real problem in his life was his heavy smoking. I thought that like most smokers who attend our clinics he would find it easy to stop after just one session.

He seemed pleased when he left the session, but after nine months I received a phone call. "Mr Carr, would you mind terribly if I came back to see you again," he said. He was convinced he understood the trap completely and, from the conversation we had, so was I. He had gone nine months without a cigarette. Obviously, he was not suffering any physical withdrawal – that goes after the first few days – but he had that feeling of "waiting for something to happen" that I described earlier. It was a chance remark as we made our farewells that helped me pinpoint the problem.

I mentioned that I would be doing a session in Paris in the spring. He said, "I find it hard to accept that I'll never be able to enjoy sitting outside a cafe in Paris in the sunshine, listening to the accordions, with a glass of wine in one hand and a Gauloise [Gauloise is a strong untipped French cigarette] in the other, watching the crowds go by." He had just described a situation that many smokers would regard as the perfect setting for their favourite cigarette. I said, "Think back to the last time you did it; were you actually consciously puffing on that Gauloise thinking, 'This smoke going into my lungs is my idea of heaven?'"

I was taken aback when he informed me that he had never been to Paris nor smoked a Gauloise! Such is the power of the brainwashing; it didn't occur to him that he was moping for a myth. I went to Paris and sat in the sunshine outside a cafe, listening to the accordions and watching the crowds go by, a glass in one hand and neither a Gauloise nor anything else in the other. It had all the charm and appeal he had described, even more so because I felt no need to choke myself to death.

DISGUSTING HABIT

Look back over your smoking years and I'm sure you can remember numerous cigarettes which tasted weird, stale or even disgusting. I remember many when I struggled for breath, or was convulsed with violent coughing fits. I also remember the embarrassment those fits caused me, and how self-conscious I felt when non-smokers gave me that quizzical look.

However, of all the hundreds of thousands of cigarettes that I smoked, I can't think of a single one when I sat there thinking, "This is my idea of heaven," or, "How lucky I am to be a smoker." I can remember meals and many other occasions when I was utterly miserable because I couldn't smoke, and how relieved I was when I was eventually allowed to light up, but that's different.

If you're honest, you'll find the only occasions you're aware of your smoking are when you want a cigarette but can't have one, or when you're smoking one but wish you didn't have to. If you continue to believe the brainwashing that you can't enjoy certain situations without a cigarette, then you won't.

The Paris cafe client had indeed understood how nicotine addiction fools smokers into believing they get a genuine crutch or pleasure from smoking, but he had failed to relate that understanding to his everyday life. He hadn't removed the brainwashing completely.

You need to analyse these situations, to understand why the cigarette appears to enhance them and that in reality it does the reverse. Instead of perpetuating the illusion by thinking, "I won't be able to enjoy such and such a situation without a cigarette," do the opposite. Remind yourself of the true position:

**_ISN'T IT MARVELLOUS, I CAN NOW ENJOY THAT
SITUATION FREE FROM THE SLAVERY OF
CHOKING MYSELF TO DEATH_**

BAD TIMES

Now let's look at the other side of the coin: the crutch. We think of the cigarette as a crutch since it appears to relieve stress. I don't mean the extreme traumas, like losing someone you love, but everyday annoyances that occur regularly in all our lives. A typical one is a car breakdown. It's late at night, pouring with rain, you're on the most dangerous part of the road, your phone has no signal and all the other drivers, instead of stopping to see if they can help, are belting past at 80mph, soaking you and hooting as if they think you've decided to stop there for the fun of it.

If you were a smoker, you would no doubt reach for a cigarette in these circumstances. The challenge arises the next time you find yourself in a similar situation after having quit. Miserable, helpless and angry, you think, "At times like this I would have had a cigarette." But look back at the last time such a trauma happened in your life and you lit up. Did it solve your problem? Did you stand there happily thinking, "It doesn't matter that I'm cold, wet, miserable and late for the most important appointment of my life, at least I've got this marvellous cigarette?" Or were you still utterly miserable?

When ex-smokers who've stopped on willpower experience these situations, they start to mope for a cigarette. They don't realise that the cigarette, far from helping, actually makes things worse. All you need to do is accept that, just as with all other non-smokers, there will be ups and downs in your life after you've quit, and understand that if you start craving a cigarette at such times, you'll be moping for an illusion, searching for something that does not exist, and creating a void. Get it clear in your mind, removing cigarettes from your life does not leave a void.

CIGARETTES CREATE A VOID, THEY DO NOT FILL IT

Ex-smokers who don't understand this suffer the misery of turning good days into bad days and making bad days worse. With Allen Carr's Easyway, you can do the opposite. If you're having a bad day, say to yourself, "OK, so today isn't so great, but at least I'm no longer a nicotine slave." If it's a good day, say, "It's great to be alive and so much nicer now that I'm a non-smoker."

SEE LIFE AS IT REALLY IS

Apart from car breakdowns, accidents and other unforeseen traumas, there are other common situations that can trigger the craving for a cigarette in the future if you're not prepared. Rather than waiting for these events to happen and hoping that, by the time they do, you will have forgotten all about smoking, it's far better to anticipate them and prepare yourself mentally. Moving house, Christmas, weddings, holidays and funerals are examples. There might be other situations that are particular to you. Ask yourself what situations might be a trigger for you, and remove the brainwashing in advance.

"I stopped smoking. I read this book by Allen Carr. Everyone who reads this book stops smoking!"

Ellen DeGeneres

ADDICTION VERSUS DEPENDENCE

So-called experts in drug addiction often use terms that in themselves create problems for addicts. The most common is "give up", which implies a sacrifice. Another is "dependence". You are only dependent on something that you cannot survive without. Nobody is ever dependent on nicotine, alcohol, heroin, cocaine, etc – people only think they are. By using the word "dependence", doctors and other so-called experts reinforce the brainwashing and confirm the addict's fears.

The terms "addiction" and "dependence" should not be confused. Diabetics might be dependent on insulin for survival, but that doesn't make them drug addicts. They have a good reason for using the drug and are in control. Addiction is the opposite. All smokers, no matter how casual, are nicotine addicts: there are no rational reasons for smoking and they are not in control.

Nicotine addiction is based on the delusion that smoking is pleasurable and relieves stress. Once you have recognised this delusion for what it is, getting free is easy.

SUMMARY

- *Remove the brainwashing completely.*

- *Once you've understood Allen Carr's Easyway, you will have no desire to smoke another cigarette.*

- *Cigarettes neither make good times better, nor help during bad times.*

- *Enjoy life more and handle stress better as a non-smoker.*

- *No one is dependent on nicotine.*

CHAPTER 15

THERE IS NOTHING TO FEAR

IN THIS CHAPTER
- *FEAR KEEPS YOU HOOKED*
- *CIGARETTES ARE YOUR ENEMY – NOT YOUR FRIEND*
- *WHEN DOES THE CRAVING GO?*
- *HANDLING THE TRIGGERS*

SEEING THE TRUE POSITION

Before we can stop smoking for good, we need to understand what is keeping us in the trap

Weigh up the advantages and disadvantages of being a smoker at any time in your life and you'll always reach the same conclusion: I'm a mug! So why do we continue to smoke? No one forces us to. Why do we close our minds to the facts?

FEAR is the driving force. It feeds on a lack of understanding, so when we find ourselves in an unfamiliar situation, fear creeps in.

The Little Nicotine Monster inside our body, which is constantly demanding its fix, creates a tiny physical aggravation. It's so slight as almost to be imperceptible, but it triggers the Big Monster in the mind: "I want a cigarette." You will now be miserable if you can't have one and that misery can lead to fear and panic. Fear is the powerful force that keeps us smoking against our better judgement and keeps the prison gates locked.

Smokers phoning our clinics to book a session are both surprised and relieved when we advise them not to attempt to quit or cut down prior to their appointment. They're even more surprised, and relieved, when we tell them to bring along an ample supply of their favourite brand as they will be able to smoke during the session.

Before we introduced smoking breaks, the session rooms had the atmosphere of an opium den. Even the most hardened smokers used to complain about the smoke. Many clients were convinced it was some form of aversion therapy. If aversion therapy worked, I would use it.

When we say, "Smoking does absolutely nothing for you whatsoever," clients tend to look at the therapist quizzically, as if to say, "So why instruct us to continue smoking until the final cigarette?"

One reason is that it's easier to remove the illusions, myths and misconceptions that keep you smoking before you get free since you can test some of them out on the spot – for example, the illusion that you enjoy the taste. In fact, why not light one now, take five or six deep puffs and ask yourself precisely what you're enjoying about it? If you're honest, you'll find it's absolutely nothing!

WHY YOU GET THE FIDGETS

Smokers feel the need for a cigarette as they sense the nicotine withdrawing from their body. If they aren't allowed to have one, they become fidgety and distracted. Remember, this lack of concentration is caused by the frustration of wanting a cigarette and not being able to have one – not being allowed to scratch the itch. Since we need our smokers to absorb the message, we ask them to carry on smoking.

Once they realise that it's just fear that prevents them from stopping, some smokers try to allay that fear by telling themselves that they always have the choice of lighting up again if they want to, that it doesn't have to be final.

However, if you start off with that attitude, you're very likely to fail sooner or later. Instead, start off with the certainty that you're going to be free forever. To achieve that certainty, we have to remove the fear and the panic first.

We have instinctive fears which protect us from the dangers of heights, fire, drowning, etc. Such fears are perfectly logical and part of our survival instinct.

However, there's nothing instinctive about the fear of stopping smoking. It's not an instinctive fear built into our DNA for our own protection.

THE FEAR OF STOPPING SMOKING IS CREATED BY STARTING SMOKING

To remove the fear of stopping smoking, approach the subject with an open mind and try to be relaxed, logical and rational. Then your fears will dissolve and you'll be a happy non-smoker from the moment you extinguish your final cigarette and remain one for the rest of your life.

YOU DECIDE

We have established that to achieve success you need to remove all doubt. Perhaps you still question whether it's possible to know for certain that something in your life will *not* happen. After all, the chances of being struck by a meteorite are infinitesimally small, yet nobody can be certain it will never happen to them. OK, I take your point. Now take mine: ex-smokers have a considerable advantage over potential meteorite victims. If a meteorite is going to hit you, there's absolutely nothing that you can do about it, whereas only you can make yourself smoke again. So the only thing you really need to worry about is yourself.

Q: WHY DOES ANYONE EVER LIGHT A CIGARETTE?
A: BECAUSE THEY WANT TO

When I extinguished my final cigarette I knew I would never get hooked again and any ex-smoker can enjoy the same freedom. All you have to do is make sure you are never again struck by the thought, "I want a cigarette", and to achieve this you must ensure that three vital points are ingrained in your mind.

1. Cigarettes do **ABSOLUTELY NOTHING** for you whatsoever. You must understand why this is so and accept it. That way, there's no feeling of deprivation.

2. You do not need to go through any transitional period (often referred to incorrectly as the "withdrawal period") before the craving goes completely. Craving is mental, not physical, and yours will be removed by the time you've finished reading this book.

3. There is no such thing as just one cigarette or occasional cigarettes. See it as it really is: the whole filthy lifetime's chain.

Some smokers find it difficult to believe they have a choice about whether to crave cigarettes or not. They labour under the misconception that you either crave something or you don't and there's nothing that can be done about it.

Fortunately they're wrong. Your body will continue to experience nicotine withdrawal for a few days after quitting, but that doesn't mean you have to be miserable or that you have to crave a cigarette.

The body is incapable of craving anything, be it food, water or rest. It is capable of experiencing hunger, thirst, tiredness, aggravation and pain, and can send messages to your brain prompting your mind to react accordingly. However, if you're asleep, your mind will not register these messages and there is no craving. It's only your conscious mind that is capable of craving because craving is a mental process.

Every smoker has the power to decide whether they are going to crave a cigarette or not. There are illusions – both conscious and unconscious – that can influence a person to crave a cigarette, but the craving itself is conscious and within your control. There is no physical craving.

It's the very use of the willpower method that makes us think we can't escape our craving. One of the mistakes we make when using willpower is we try not to think about smoking, with the result that we end up obsessed by it.

Trying not to think about something is a mug's game anyway. If I say to you now, "Don't think about elephants," what are you immediately thinking about?

GRIEVING FOR NOTHING

Many smokers suffer the illusion they can never get completely free. I was convinced cigarettes were my

> friend, my confidence, my courage, part of my identity. I
> feared that if I ever stopped smoking, I would not only lose
> a companion, but also a part of myself.

If you lose a friend, you mourn. When you get over the initial tragedy and life goes on, you're left with a genuine void in your life that you can never completely fill. But there's nothing you can do about it. You have no choice but to accept the situation and eventually you do.

When smokers, alcoholics, heroin and other drug addicts stop by using the willpower method, they feel they've lost a friend. They know they're making the correct decision, but there's still a feeling of sacrifice and therefore a void in their lives. This isn't a genuine void, but if they believe it's genuine, the effect is the same. What's more, this particular friend isn't dead! On the contrary, the tobacco industry, other smokers and society in general ensure that those whingeing ex-smokers are subjected to the ever-present temptation of forbidden fruit for the rest of their lives.

However, when you get rid of your mortal enemy, the cigarette, there's no need to mourn. On the contrary, you can rejoice and celebrate from the start, and you can continue to rejoice and celebrate for the rest of your life. Get it clear in your mind: the cigarette is not your friend and never has been. It's the worst enemy you've ever had. You are sacrificing nothing, just making marvellous positive gains.

So the answer to the question, "When will the craving go?" is: "Whenever you choose." You could spend the next few days, and possibly the rest of your life, continuing to believe that cigarettes were your friend and wondering when you'll stop missing them. If you do that, you'll feel miserable, the craving may never go and you'll either feel deprived for the rest of your life or more likely end up smoking again and feeling even worse.

Alternatively, you could recognise the cigarette for the enemy it really is. Then, you need neither crave a cigarette nor wait for anything to happen. Instead, whenever you think about smoking, you can celebrate: "Yippee! I'm a non-smoker!"

CALL TIME ON A LIFETIME'S BRAINWASHING

I asked you to approach this process with a relaxed, rational and open mind because that helps you understand the nicotine trap and deal with the Little Nicotine Monster inside your body. During the first few days after your final cigarette, the Little Monster will be sending messages to your brain that it wants you to interpret as "I want a cigarette." But you now understand the true situation and, instead of having one, or getting uptight because you mustn't have one, pause for a moment. Take a deep breath. There's no need to panic. There is no pain. The feeling isn't so bad. It's what smokers suffer throughout their smoking lives.

RE-PROGRAMME YOUR BRAIN

In the past your mind interpreted the withdrawal pangs of the Little Monster as "I want a cigarette" because it had every reason to believe that a cigarette would satisfy the empty, insecure feeling. But now you understand that, far from relieving that feeling, the cigarette caused it. So just relax, accept the feeling for what it really is and remind yourself, "Non-smokers don't have this problem. This is what smokers suffer, and they suffer it throughout their smoking lives. Isn't it great! It will soon be gone forever." That way the withdrawal pangs cease to feel like withdrawal pangs and become moments of pleasure.

You might find that, particularly during the first few days, you forget that you've quit. It can happen at any time. It's often first thing in the morning when you're still half asleep. You think, "I'll get up and have a cigarette." Then you remember you're now a non-smoker.

> A permanent psychological battle rages between smokers and ex-smokers and it helps to be prepared for your own reactions, and to understand theirs. As the ex-smoker you hold all the cards. Smokers are painfully aware of that. However, if unprepared, an ex-smoker can be bluffed into believing that the reverse is true.

Another occasion might be when you're socializing. You're chatting away and suddenly there's a pack of cigarettes under your nose. You may automatically reach for one, then catch yourself. Such times can be make or break, particularly if the friend who is offering the cigarette reacts before you do and says, "I thought you'd stopped." There you stand, hand suspended in mid-air. It can be disconcerting. The smokers around you can't hide their delight. To them this is proof you haven't kicked it and they're convinced you're dying for a cigarette.

Such situations can be disastrous if you react in the wrong way. Doubts can surface and you may start to question your decision and lose faith in yourself. Prepare for these situations so that you remain calm and instead of thinking, "I can't have one," simply think, "Isn't it great, I don't need to smoke anymore. I'm free!"

Remember, ex-smokers will be envying you because every single one of them will be wishing they could be like you – **FREE FROM THE WHOLE FILTHY NIGHTMARE**.

The mental associations between a cigarette and a drink, the end of the meal, etc can linger on long after the physical withdrawal has ceased and this undermines the attempts of smokers who quit using the willpower method. In their minds they have built up a massive case against smoking, have decided to become a non-smoker, have managed to go for however long without smoking and yet on certain occasions a little voice keeps saying, "I want a cigarette." This is because they still think of the cigarette as a pleasure and a crutch.

Although you will no longer suffer the illusion that you're being deprived, it's still imperative that you prepare yourself for these situations. Whether they're first thing in the morning, or you're returning to an empty house, or you're in the company of smokers, rejoice that you can now either enjoy or handle these moments without choking yourself to death. If you momentarily forget that you no longer smoke, that isn't a bad sign, on the contrary, it's a very good one. It's certain proof that your life is returning to the happy state you were in before you got hooked, when smoking didn't dominate your whole existence.

Expecting these moments to happen, and being prepared for them, means you won't be caught off guard. You'll be wearing a suit of impenetrable armour. You know you've made the correct decision and nobody will be able to make you doubt it. That way, instead of being the cause of your downfall, these moments can give you strength, security and immense pleasure and remind you just how wonderful it is to be **FREE**.

SUMMARY

- *Remove the brainwashing and you remove the fears that keep you trapped.*

- *Cigarettes are not your friend, they are your mortal enemy.*

- *The craving for cigarettes is mental not physical.*

- *Be relaxed, rational and open-minded and you'll find it easy to get free.*

- *Be prepared for the triggers and you'll find it easy to stay free.*

CHAPTER 16

TAKING CONTROL

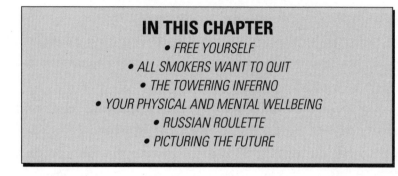

IN THIS CHAPTER
- *FREE YOURSELF*
- *ALL SMOKERS WANT TO QUIT*
- *THE TOWERING INFERNO*
- *YOUR PHYSICAL AND MENTAL WELLBEING*
- *RUSSIAN ROULETTE*
- *PICTURING THE FUTURE*

A LIFE IN SHACKLES

Throughout their lives smokers are well aware of the many powerful reasons to stop. In most cases it's only with hindsight that we fully appreciate the greatest gain from quitting: to escape from slavery

Though I denied it to myself, I clearly knew I wasn't in control of my smoking. I felt in control of every other aspect of my life, but allowed cigarettes to control me. I was a slave to something I detested and despised. It made me angry and this was the real reason for my desperation to quit. And yet I still wasn't aware of just how powerless I had become as a smoker until I had been a non-smoker for several months.

So intent are we on resisting all the people who are trying to make us quit and searching for any flimsy excuse that will allow us to smoke just one more cigarette, that we close our minds to the terrible evils of being a smoker and we refuse to confront what is probably the greatest evil of all: the sheer slavery.

Health is the most common reason smokers give for wanting to quit but again we try to block our minds to the health risks and kid ourselves that it won't happen to us.

Money is another common reason for quitting. As a chain-smoker I spent the price of a luxury car on tobacco. Nowadays that's what the average 20–a-day smoker in the UK spends in their lifetime. That's a huge sum, but the real sense of achievement quitting brought was not so much the improved health and wealth, which were great in themselves, but no longer having to regard myself as a slave.

When smokers are asked why they smoke, their reactions are nearly always defensive and negative. They can't seem to find reasons why they do, but resort to excuses for why they haven't stopped yet.

"I can afford it."

"I haven't noticed any deterioration in my health."

"I haven't got any other vices."

Now compare those to the answers you get if you ask someone why they play football, or go to the cinema, or visit art galleries, or listen to music. When something gives you genuine pleasure, you're only too keen to enthuse about it. You don't make excuses for why you don't stop doing it!

The Times newspaper wrote, "Allen Carr's method logically reverses all the myths and excuses that smokers give to justify their smoking." That's true. However, what really enables smokers to get free with this method is the realisation that they need not be a slave to cigarettes: they won't miss smoking, they will enjoy life more, they will deal better with stress, they won't have to go through some terrible trauma in order to escape.

ALL SMOKERS WANT TO QUIT

Many people, smokers and non-smokers alike, dispute this fact. One of the interesting things that emerged from the massive marketing campaigns for nicotine products such as patches and gums, and for Zyban and Champix, was the number of smokers who were lured into trying them. Where did they all suddenly appear from? If smokers didn't want to quit, why would the patches, gums and pills have created such massive interest? Why would the stop-smoking industry be worth billions of pounds and why would my stop-smoking organization have spread across the globe purely by word of mouth without any advertising?

The reason is that, whether it's openly or secretly, all smokers want to stop. They were waiting for some magic pill that would enable them to get free and, even though the nicotine products Zyban and Champix turned out not to be the magic pills they were seeking, many smokers were prepared to risk hundreds of pounds in case they might be. Surveys show that over 70% of smokers say that they want to quit. The other 30% just won't admit it. After all, it sounds less pathetic to say, "I smoke because I choose to and have no desire to stop," than "I'm a miserable addict and would give anything to quit, but I just haven't got the willpower." Smoking parents are dead against their children smoking. Why? Because they wish they'd never started themselves which means, given the choice, they'd rather be non-smokers. In my first book, *The Easy Way to Stop Smoking*, I offered so-called confirmed smokers – those who claim to have no intention of stopping – free cigarettes for the rest of their life if they gave me the money they would spend on cigarettes in just one year. The book has sold over 10 million copies and yet no one has taken me up on that offer because no one is prepared to sentence themselves to the nightmare of remaining a smoker for the rest of their life. Every single smoker, openly or secretly, consciously or unconsciously, would love to be in the position you are going to be in when you've finished this book – **FREE**.

"Allen Carr's Easy Way to Stop Smoking – if you or someone you know wants to quit, buy this book. It worked for me and about 20 other people I know. Seriously."

Jason Mraz, Singer-songwriter

Smoking is now seen as antisocial and it's not just attitudes and manners that have changed, it's the whole paraphernalia. Gold lighters have been replaced by disposables. There was a time when the standard 18th or 21st birthday present was an expensive lighter or cigarette case. Nowadays you rarely see them. All smokers are thinking short term. They all want to quit.

ALL SMOKERS WOULD RATHER BE NON-SMOKERS

Society regards smokers as weak-willed, but the evidence does not support this conclusion. On the contrary, smokers who continue to smoke despite the massive pressures to stop tend to be dominant individuals who refuse to be controlled by others. Nor do they like being controlled by cigarettes that they loathe and despise. I can't tell you how nice it is to be free from that slavery, that domination. To be able to look at other smokers, not with envy or a feeling of deprivation, but with genuine pity, as you would look at any other drug addict. The greatest gain from becoming a non-smoker is not so much the health or the money – although they are fantastic bonuses – it's no longer to loathe or despise yourself for being the slave to something you detest, to have set yourself free!

THE HEALTH FACTOR

When we start to talk about health at the clinics, some smokers think, "Here comes the shock treatment." I assure you we do not use shock treatment – it doesn't work.

While explaining how smoking hinders concentration, we sometimes ask, "Which organ in your body has the greatest need of a good supply of blood?" The stupid grins, usually on the faces of the men, often indicate they've missed the point.

However, they're not entirely wrong. I have no intention of going into detail about the adverse effect that smoking had on my own sexual performance, or that of other ex-smokers with whom I have discussed the subject. Suffice it to say that I attributed my dwindling sexual prowess and activity to advancing years. I was wrong. I had no idea until after I had stopped, but I later learned that smoking can lead to impotence. I can also assure you that when you're fit and healthy, you'll enjoy sex more, for much longer, and more often. The deterioration in one's sex life may appear one of the more trivial of the smoking-related health issues, but I can assure you it makes a huge difference to one's quality of life when it improves again!

THE TOWERING INFERNO

Being a smoker is like being trapped in a burning building. You have only two frightening alternatives: jump or stay inside and hope for rescue. Only when the fear of burning or suffocating becomes greater than the fear of jumping will you make your move.

For the smoker there is the fear of continuing to smoke and all that involves – the diseases, the money, the slavery, etc – on one side, and the fear of stopping on the other. Just as the person in the building won't jump until it becomes absolutely essential, so smokers instinctively put off what they see as the dreadful day, hoping that they will be miraculously rescued before they contract one of the killer diseases.

But the subtlety of the smoking trap puts the smoker at a distinct disadvantage to the person in the inferno. The person in the burning building cannot close his mind to his predicament. The threat is clear and present, whereas the smoker's risk isn't immediately apparent. Furthermore, smokers try to block their minds to the problem: "It won't happen to me", or "I'll stop before it reaches that stage – I'm not a complete idiot." So there seems to be no pressing need to solve the problem today and so the natural tendency is not to do so. The trouble is, the chances are it *will* happen to you. There's a more than 50% chance you will die as a direct result of smoking, unless you stop.

Non-smokers find it difficult to understand why smokers are prepared to take these tremendous risks for the dubious pleasure of breathing poisonous fumes into their lungs. And why would someone continue to smoke after watching a loved one suffer a protracted, painful and degrading death from lung cancer? I've stated before that smokers are often strong-willed. It's the same determination combined with delusion that makes them carry on.

You might part with your hard-earned money every week in return for a one in 14 million chance of winning the lottery in the hope that "It could be you". Yet when told there's a more than one in two chance that smoking will kill you, you remain convinced that "It won't be you".

When tragedy does happen, we turn the excuse round: "It's pointless stopping now. I've left it too late!"

Because we're in denial, we're not even aware of most of the cigarettes we smoke and think of smoking as "just a habit". If every time we lit a cigarette we had to face the fact that it was going to cost us the price of a house and could be the one to trigger cancer in our lungs, the illusion of pleasure would disappear.

Even when we manage to block our mind to the dire consequences of our addiction, we still sense we're being stupid. If we had to face up to it, the whole process would become intolerable.

YOUR CIGARETTES OR YOUR LEGS!

It's not difficult to see why smokers close their ears to the horrific statistics, but what most people find impossible to understand is how a smoker can keep smoking after a doctor has said to them, "If you don't stop, you will lose your legs." This is not a shock tactic, I just want you to understand how any smoker can get to that stage and still not quit. No doubt you're convinced that, faced with that choice, you would stop. You need to understand why you might not.

Amazingly, around half of all smokers are unaware that smoking can cause of loss of limbs. I can remember wondering how anyone could possibly allow their legs to be amputated rather than quit. Arthur Askey, the old music hall comedian, had to have his legs amputated as a direct result of smoking and still didn't quit. When I heard the news, this thought honestly went through my head: "At his age, are legs really essential? You can survive without legs. But cigarettes, they are absolutely essential!" Such is the effect of addiction on the brain. I later came up with another explanation: that smokers like Arthur Askey were freak cases. It didn't dawn on me that I was one of them. I knew that smoking was going to kill me and I still hadn't stopped.

We don't understand why we smoke and at first we feel no reason to stop. Once we realise it's killing us, costing us a fortune and controlling our life, we begin to feel more and more in need of what we perceive as our little crutch.

Bad health or lack of money might help you abstain for a while, but if you still have a desire to smoke, sooner or later you'll fall back into the trap again.

Eventually, the debilitating effects of the addiction and the poisoning have dragged you down so far, both physically and mentally, that even though you know it's killing you, you become resigned to your fate. What demonic force warps the mind of the smoker, driving them to bury their head in the sand and convincing them that it's better to lose their limbs or even their life rather than quit?

ADDICTION!

This force is addiction and it's fuelled by the fear that we can't enjoy or cope with life without cigarettes. Non-smokers don't suffer this fear. Nicotine doesn't relieve it, it causes it. It's fantastic to be free of this fear.

Once you're enjoying life more and coping better with stress as a non-smoker, you'll no longer have to block your mind to the health scares. On the contrary, one of the huge bonuses of quitting is that you no longer need to worry about them.

Lung cancer, heart disease, arteriosclerosis, emphysema, angina, thrombosis, bronchitis, asthma – these are terrible diseases and it's scandalous that society allows millions of smokers to suffer protracted, painful and premature deaths because of them.

Stop saying, "It won't happen to me," thereby ensuring that it does. Start thinking, "It will happen to me," thereby ensuring that it doesn't!

ILL EFFECTS

It is now clear that all sorts of diseases are caused by smoking, including diabetes, cervical cancer and breast cancer. Several of the adverse effects that smoking had on my health, many of which I had been suffering from for years, didn't become apparent to me until years after I had stopped.

It didn't occur to me that, because smoking blocks the capillaries, I was on the way to arteriosclerosis myself. I thought my grey complexion was natural. I had varicose veins in my thirties and about five years before I quit I developed a strange sensation in my legs at night. I would occasionally get violent pains in my chest which I feared must be lung cancer but later realised was angina. All these ailments miraculously disappeared when I quit.

When I was a child I bled profusely from cuts. As an adult, I hardly bled at all. When I cut myself, a browny-red gunge oozed out of me. The colour worried me. I knew that blood was meant to be bright red and I thought I must have some sort of blood disease. Not until after I had stopped did I learn that smoking coagulates the blood and that the brownish colour was due to lack of oxygen.

In hindsight, it was this effect that smoking was having on my health that most fills me with horror. When I think of my poor heart trying to pump that gunge around restricted blood vessels, day in, day out, without missing a single beat, I find it a miracle that I didn't suffer a stroke or a heart attack. It made me realise what an incredible machine the body is!

I had liver spots on my hands in my forties. I tried to ignore them, assuming that they were due to premature ageing caused by my hectic lifestyle. A smoker, whose brother had recommended the Raynes Park clinic, remarked that when his brother stopped his liver spots had disappeared. I looked at my hands; to my amazement mine had gone too.

Dots used to flash in front of my eyes if I stood up too quickly and I felt dizzy as if I were about to black out. I never related this to smoking. I assumed it was quite normal and that it happened to everyone else. Not until long after I had quit and another ex-smoker told me that he no longer had that sensation did I realise I no longer had it either.

We're fooled into believing smoking helps us enjoy life when in reality it does the opposite. As a youngster, I was shocked when I heard my smoking father say that he had no wish to live beyond fifty. Little did I realise that I would come to suffer the same lack of *joie de vivre*.

STUCK IN A MINEFIELD

Smoking is like walking around a minefield. As a smoker you remain in the minefield for the rest of your life. Perhaps you think that's just life? After all, they say, the only certainty in life is death and it could strike at any moment. If we spent our lives worrying about it, we would be miserable.

Smokers apply the same logic to their smoking. "I've got to die of something, so what's the point in worrying about it?" The problem is that as a smoker you're *not* going through life carefree, untroubled by the possibility of a premature and painful death which is entirely self-inflicted; you *are* worrying about it – that's why you've decided to do something about it.

Another subtlety of the trap which helps us block our minds to the killer diseases is that we make the mistake of thinking that, provided we don't actually contract one of them, we'll get away scot-free – like playing Russian roulette. I knew smoking made me short of breath, cough and congested my lungs, but I didn't think of these as diseases or of myself as being ill.

DEATH CREEPING UP ON US?

The deterioration in our physical and mental health caused by smoking is usually gradual and so, like getting older, we scarcely notice it. The face we see in the mirror each day appears identical to the face we peered at the day before. It's only when we look at an old photograph that ageing becomes apparent.

The imperceptibility of the ageing processes is one of the many kindnesses of nature, but this subtlety isn't kind to smokers because it prevents them from seeing what they're doing to themselves. Those who are lucky enough to appear healthy tend to take it for granted, but you never know what's going on beneath the skin.

Smoking progressively clogs up your veins and arteries, and starves every cell in your body of oxygen and other nutrients, replacing them with over 4,000 chemicals and over 100 different poisons which prevent every part of your body from operating efficiently. Like AIDS, it gradually destroys your immune system. Smokers who are HIV positive contract full-blown AIDS twice as quickly as non-smokers.

If only it were possible to give every smoker a preview of how they would feel after just three weeks of freedom. They'd think, "Wow! Will I really feel this great?" Not only would they notice a substantial improvement in their physical health and energy, but also in their courage, confidence and self-respect.

After quitting, I occasionally had nightmares that I was smoking again. This is quite common among ex-smokers. Some worry that it means they're still subconsciously pining for a cigarette. Don't worry about it. The fact that it was a nightmare means you're happy not to be a smoker.

When you get free, you come out of a dark world of anxiety, depression and slavery and into a technicolour world of health, sunshine and freedom.

SUMMARY

- *Freedom is the greatest gain from stopping.*

- *All smokers want to quit.*

- *Stop denying you're in denial.*

- *The fear of life without cigarettes keeps us smoking despite the terrible consequences.*

- *You only have one body – look after it.*

- *Look forward to the thrill of being a non-smoker!*

CHAPTER 17

WITHDRAWAL

IN THIS CHAPTER
- *NICOTINE WITHDRAWAL CAUSES NO PHYSICAL PAIN*
- *COSTING A PACKET*
- *THAT PANIC FEELING*
- *KILLING THE LITTLE NICOTINE MONSTER*
- *WILLPOWER – THE ETERNAL TORTURE*
- *THE FEELING OF FREEDOM*
- *PREPARING FOR YOUR FINAL CIGARETTE*

NO NEED FOR FEAR

*Smokers talk of the torture of withdrawal. But how bad is
the pain, and where does it actually hurt?*

I have explained that the physical withdrawal pangs from
nicotine are so slight that you can hardly feel them. I have also
stated that the only reason a smoker lights a cigarette is to relieve
the withdrawal. If the pangs are almost imperceptible, why do
smokers find it so difficult to quit with other methods?

Consider this: how can smokers sleep peacefully for eight
hours without a cigarette, then wake up and not be in agony after
such a long period of abstinence? If the physical withdrawal were

so bad, it would wake them up during the night. Most smokers get out of bed before lighting up; many don't smoke until after breakfast; some even wait until they've left for work before they light their first cigarette. Not only are they getting by quite happily without any physical pain, they're not even aware of any discomfort.

Of course, they'll be looking forward to their first cigarette. If you were brave enough to snatch the cigarette from their lips as they went to light it, they would probably get extremely irate. But that's not a reaction to physical pain; it's mental panic triggered by the prospect of being deprived of a pleasure or crutch. The pangs recede when they know their next smoke is taken care of. If it were genuine physical pain, it would be there all the time, like toothache.

The panic starts before you even run out of cigarettes. How often have you been out late at night and calculated, "I reckon I'll be up about another four hours, but I've only got about an hour's supply left!" The panic intensifies as you smoke the last one. Nicotine is flowing into your body, yet to you it feels like nicotine withdrawal pangs.

"Someone gave me Allen Carr's book. I found it very useful. It's a great book."

Lou Reed

COSTING A PACKET

Most smokers start to panic when they get down to the last few cigarettes in the packet. I used to panic when I got down to my last few packets! I wasn't happy playing a round of golf unless I had three full packs on me. Even on the windiest of days I could only smoke 40 cigarettes per round, so why did I need three packs? Because in the days when I only carried two, I dropped one in a puddle and it got soaked. I like to feel that I learn from my mistakes, so from then on I carried at least three packets to cover all eventualities!

THE PANIC-FREE SMOKER

When we refer to "that panic feeling" at group sessions, most smokers nod knowingly. But occasionally a heavy smoker says, "I'm sorry, I don't know what you mean." The rest of the group will look at him with surprise.

Those looks become incredulous when we later remark that smokers will smoke camel dung rather than nothing, and the same smoker says, "I can't agree with you. If I couldn't get my own brand, I wouldn't smoke anything."

We know that all drug addicts have to lie to themselves, but we generally find that smokers at our clinics like being honest and purging their conscience. If these brand-loyal smokers were telling the truth, it seemed to contradict what we were saying about the nicotine trap.

However, the reason these heavy smokers don't get the panic

feeling is because they make sure they avoid it. They're so frightened of getting it, they take every precaution to ensure they never get low on cigarettes.

So while they might well believe that it's their chosen brand or nothing, they've never put it to the test. They're not lying, nor are they telling the truth. Despite what they might think, *every* smoker who is denied cigarettes experiences the panic feeling. But remember:

WITHDRAWAL FROM NICOTINE CAUSES NO PHYSICAL PAIN

Even if it did, pain isn't the great evil in life. We're very well equipped to deal with it. Try squeezing your thigh and digging your nails in, gradually increasing the pressure. You'll find you can endure quite a severe level of pain without any accompanying fear or panic. That's because you're in control. You know the cause of the pain and you know you can end it whenever you choose.

Now repeat the exercise, and when the pain is as much as you can bear, try to imagine that it wasn't you causing it but that it had just suddenly appeared and that you knew neither the cause, nor how long it would last. Now imagine that pain being in your head, ears or chest. You would be in an instant state of panic. The problem is not pain, it's the fear and panic that pain can provoke if you don't understand why you're feeling it or know what the consequences might be.

SMOKERS SUFFER NICOTINE WITHDRAWAL PANGS ALL THE TIME

The generally held belief is that smokers who try to quit have to endure a terrible trauma caused by withdrawal from nicotine. In fact, they suffer nicotine withdrawal their entire smoking life.

Watch smokers, particularly when they're not allowed to smoke. They'll be restless; one hand will be fidgeting near their mouth; their feet will be twitching; or if everything else is still, they'll be grinding their teeth. I call it the smokers' twitch. It's triggered by an empty, insecure feeling which can quickly turn into frustration, irritation, anxiety, fear and panic if they can't smoke.

Get it clear in your mind: you don't need to feel at all deprived when you stop as long as you realise that cigarettes cause rather than relieve the feeling. If you carry on smoking, you'll suffer that empty, insecure feeling for the rest of your life.

FAILURE OF THE WILL

Smokers who try to quit using the willpower method *do* suffer terrible trauma. I have experienced this and, as I described earlier, it reduced me to tears on more than one occasion. So if it's not physical, what is it and how can we deal with it? What causes the panic and fear that keep smokers in the trap, to the extent that they'll have limbs amputated rather than stop?

> Ignorance and illusion are the twin evils that combine to turn a small signal in your body into panic and torture in your mind.

Imagine having an itch that you're not allowed to scratch, an itch that lasts not just a few seconds, but is constant. Imagine the state you would be in and the tremendous willpower you would have to exert to resist scratching that itch just once. Furthermore, imagine that you believed the itch would last for the rest of your life unless you scratched it.

How long do you think you could last before you scratched that itch? And if you did manage to go a week without scratching it, imagine the sense of relief you would feel when you finally gave in. That's the torture ex-smokers suffer on the willpower method.

Long after their body has recovered from nicotine withdrawal, every time these ex-smokers finish a meal, or are bored, or suffer stress, or need to concentrate, they still believe they're being deprived. The fact it's an illusion doesn't prevent them from having a mental itch they can no longer scratch by having a cigarette.

You simply have to realise that the perception of the cigarette as a pleasure or crutch is a figment of your imagination, a leftover from the brainwashing. Why did I find it so easy to stop when I extinguished my final cigarette? Because I realised that the empty, insecure feeling of wanting a cigarette was caused by the last cigarette I smoked, and that the one thing that would ensure that

I would suffer that feeling for the rest of my life would be to smoke another.

Why didn't I suffer as I had on previous attempts? Because that torture and misery was caused by the belief that I was being deprived. When I realised that the crutch or pleasure was just an illusion, there was no sense of deprivation and, consequently, no misery or torture. On the contrary, there was just a **FEELING OF FREEDOM**.

WITHDRAWING WITH CONFIDENCE

After extinguishing the final cigarette your body will continue to withdraw from nicotine for a few days. How do you handle it? I emphasise that, although the physical withdrawal is so slight that it's almost imperceptible, you should not ignore it. It's essential that you are aware that, when you lit your first cigarette, you created an evil Little Monster inside your body, like a tapeworm, except that this monster feeds on only one substance: a powerful poison called nicotine. As soon as you cut off the supply of nicotine, you have done the one thing necessary to purge your body of that evil monster.

> From the moment you cut off the supply of nicotine, the Little Monster begins to die. In its death throes it will try to entice you to feed it. Think of it as a parasite. Create a mental image of it and enjoy starving it to death.

Be aware of the Little Nicotine Monster, and make sure you do not respond to its death throes by thinking, "I want a cigarette." See it clearly for what it is: an empty, insecure feeling *caused* by the last cigarette. The feeling itself isn't pleasant, but you will feel marvellous because you understand the cause and know that the Little Monster inside you is dying. Take a sadistic delight in those death throes. Even if you do get that feeling of "I want a cigarette" for a few days, don't worry about it. See it for what it is, the Little Monster trying to tempt you to feed it. You now have complete control over it. It's no longer destroying you: you are destroying it and soon you'll be free forever.

HOW LONG BEFORE I'M CURED?

I bet you're thinking, "OK, but how soon?" Nicotine is a fast-acting drug which leaves the body in a matter of hours. However, what's relevant here is the time it takes an addict's body to stop experiencing the last traces of withdrawal. Your body will continue to withdraw from nicotine for just a few days after extinguishing your final cigarette. The physical withdrawal is noticeable for a maximum of only five days after which the Little Monster dies.

Smokers using the willpower method tend to find that their minds are initially completely obsessed with not being allowed to smoke. Then, usually after around three weeks, comes a moment when they suddenly realise that they have not thought about smoking for a while. It's clean slipped their mind. This is a dangerous moment. The belief that life will always be miserable without smoking is replaced by the belief that time will solve the problem. They think this is a breakthrough and feel like celebrating. What possible harm could it do to reward themselves with just one cigarette?

If they're stupid enough to light one, it will taste weird and give no illusion of support or pleasure. Remember, the only reason any smoker believes the cigarette gives them pleasure or a crutch is that, when they light up, it partially relieves the symptoms of withdrawal and they feel more relaxed.

The ex-smoker who is no longer withdrawing from nicotine will not suffer that illusion because there's no physical withdrawal to relieve.

However, they have now put nicotine back into their body. The nicotine will leave their body and doubt will enter their mind. One little voice will be saying, "That tasted awful." Another will be saying, "Maybe, but I'd like another one." They will usually resist having another one immediately. There's no way they want to get hooked again, so they allow what they consider to be a safe period to pass.

The next time they're tempted, they can now say to themselves, "I smoked one last time and didn't get hooked, so what's the harm in having another?" Ring any bells? They're just falling into the same trap yet again!

I emphasise that these observations relate solely to the willpower method. When you quit with Allen Carr's Easyway, you will not feel deprived and you will be completely free.

THE MOMENT OF TRUTH

You might well believe that you have understood everything, but how can you know? We've learned from the feedback we receive that some smokers misunderstand several of the points we make, yet still find it relatively easy to stop.

They sometimes say, "It was just as you said it would be; it was hard for the first five days, then it was ridiculously easy." We never say that. On the contrary, we emphasise that right from the moment you extinguish your final cigarette it can be easy and enjoyable to quit .

In any case, there are many factors which can come into play here. It might be that the five days following your final cigarette were good days for other reasons. You think, "What's so difficult about this?" Then you have one of those days that both non-smokers and smokers occasionally have, when absolutely everything that can go wrong does. It has nothing to do with the fact that you've stopped smoking, but remember: nicotine withdrawal feels identical to everyday hunger and stress, and these can act as triggers for a cigarette.

This is one of the reasons that smokers using the willpower method are never quite sure when they've kicked it. Hunger and stress make such ex-smokers think, "I need a cigarette!" In reality a cigarette wouldn't even give the illusion of partially relieving the feeling, but how are they to know that? On the contrary, they're still convinced that a cigarette would help. The genuine stress is now increased because they believe that they are being deprived of a crutch that will ease the situation.

It's Catch 22. They can either go through the rest of their lives believing they're missing out, or they can find out for sure. Unfortunately, the only way they can do that is to light a cigarette. Their stress is not relieved – in fact it's increased by their sense of disappointment at having given in to temptation – and the inevitable outcome is that pretty soon they'll be smoking just as before.

SOON YOU'RE GOING TO SMOKE YOUR VERY FINAL CIGARETTE

If this thought still causes you panic, remember: the tobacco companies depend on that fear and panic to keep you hooked. Also remember: nicotine doesn't relieve fear or panic, it causes them. Compose yourself for a moment. Is there really any reason to panic? Nothing bad can happen because you stop smoking.

You will do something that you have already done thousands of times before: extinguish a cigarette. This particular cigarette will be a very, very special one, for the simple reason that it will be your last.

In a few days you will feel physically and mentally stronger. You'll have more money, more energy, more confidence and more self-respect. It's essential not to wait three weeks, five days or even five seconds to become a non-smoker.

This is one of the main reasons that smokers using the willpower method find it so difficult. What are they waiting for? To find out if they'll ever smoke again? They're waiting not to do something... waiting, waiting, for the rest of their lives.

You become a non-smoker the moment you extinguish your final cigarette. Remember what we are achieving is a frame of mind. Begin with a feeling of excitement, of relief that the whole filthy nightmare is now finally over and of elation that you are now free. Enjoy being a non-smoker right from the start.

SUMMARY

- *The trauma of withdrawal is mental rather than physical and Allen Carr's Easyway removes it.*

- *Recognise the physical withdrawal for what it is and it's easy to deal with.*

- *Be aware that everyday hunger and stress feel the same as nicotine withdrawal, but a cigarette will not relieve them.*

- *Smokers suffer withdrawal pangs all the time. Non-smokers do not suffer them.*

- *Get into a positive frame of mind: feel the excitement of what you are achieving!*

CHAPTER 18

THE FINAL CIGARETTE

IN THIS CHAPTER
• THE **RATIONALISED** CHECKLIST • CHOOSING YOUR MOMENT
• YOUR FINAL CIGARETTE • DEATH THROES OF THE LITTLE MONSTER
• THE INSTRUCTIONS

THE RIGHT TIME TO QUIT

*You've now received virtually all the information you need
to quit easily, painlessly and permanently, so how do you
choose your moment?*

By now your attitude to quitting should be: "Great! There's no
reason to smoke any more."

If you're not yet in that frame of mind, it means you've missed
the point somewhere. Review the summaries at the end of each
chapter and use our code word, **RATIONALISED**, see overleaf to
help you recap.

RATIONALISED is both a reminder and a checklist. Go
through each item and ask yourself, "Do I understand it? Do
I agree with it? Do I believe it? Am I following it?"

If you have any doubts, re-read the relevant chapters.

R	**REJOICE!** *There's nothing to give up.* *Chapters 1, 2, 3, 4, 5, 7, 9, 11, 14, 15.*
A	**ADVICE** *Ignore it if it conflicts with Allen Carr's Easyway.* *Chapters 2, 3, 6, 7, 8, 10, 14.*
T	**TIMING** *Today!* *Chapter 14, 15, 17, 18.*
I	**IMMEDIATE** *You're free when you put out your final cigarette.* *Chapters 2, 4, 5, 14, 17.*
O	**ONE CIGARETTE** *will cost you x* pounds and kill you! [See right.]* *Chapter 4, 5, 8, 12, 13, 16, 18.*
N	**NEVER** *smoke or even crave a cigarette.* *Chapters 3, 4, 9, 15, 17.*
A	**ADDICTIVE PERSONALITY** *There's no such thing.* *Chapter 8.*
L	**LIFESTYLE** *Don't change it unless you want to.* *Chapter 12, 18.*
I	**INTAKE** *Nothing containing nicotine.* *Chapter 11, 12.*
S	**SUBSTITUTES** *Don't use them, they don't work.* *Chapters 2, 11, 12.*
E	**ELEPHANTS** *Don't try not to think about smoking.* *Chapter 15, 18.*
D	**DON'T DOUBT YOUR DECISION.** *Chapters 14, 16, 17, 18.*

* To calculate the amount smoking would cost you if you continued, smokers who average 20 a day should deduct their age from 60 and multiply the remaining years by £2,200 ($3,500). If you're over 60, you have no need to worry about the cost; if you continue to smoke, it's not likely that you will live long enough for the cost to be significant.

ALL YOU NEED TO DO IS FOLLOW THE INSTRUCTIONS AND YOU WILL SUCCEED

If you believe you're different from the millions of other ex-smokers in the world, as I once did, then you're just being stupid, as I once was.

You have already done all the hard work necessary to reach the right frame of mind. Your training and preparation are almost complete.

You are fully equipped to succeed at something which most ex-smokers recognise as the most important and significant achievement of their lives.

You may now have a feeling of impatience and excitement, like a dog straining at the leash and, if so, that's great. However, you still need to focus carefully on the rest of this book.

Shortly, you'll be smoking your final cigarette. When should you do it?

MEANINGLESS DAYS

Two types of occasions often trigger attempts to quit. One is a traumatic event such as a health scare. The other is a day such as New Year's Day or National No Smoking Day. I call them meaningless because they have no relation to your smoking other than to provide a target day to stop. There would be nothing wrong with that if it helped, but meaningless days cause more harm than good.

According to its organisers, vast numbers of smokers quit on National No Smoking Day. In fact it's the one day any self-respecting smoker will refuse to stop. Many smoke twice as many, twice as blatantly. Smokers resent lectures from do-gooders who have no understanding of smoking.

New Year's Day is by far the most popular meaningless day and has the lowest success rate. We usually smoke so much around Christmas and New Year that we wake up each morning with a mouth like a cesspit. By New Year's Eve our chests are so congested that we're only too pleased to make a resolution. After a few days of abstinence, we've recovered from the celebrations and are feeling better for not smoking, but the Little Monster is crying out for its fix and as we don't understand that smoking, far from solving the problem, will simply perpetuate it, we pick up a cigarette, and another and another.

Meaningless days encourage us to go through the motions of half-hearted attempts to quit, only to suffer a period of deprivation followed by failure that ingrains in our mind how difficult it is to stop. Our willpower is exhausted and it's not until the fear of stopping is outweighed by the desire to stop that we resolve to make another attempt.

All our lives as smokers, we desperately search for ways to put off the evil day. Meaningless days merely provide us with an excuse to postpone our attempt to quit until the next meaningless day, when we fail again anyway.

Then there are those events we had always assured ourselves would make us quit on the spot, like health scares. Ironically, these stressful times are also when we feel we most need what we've been fooled into regarding as our little crutch. And this is yet another ingenuity of the smoking trap:

NO MATTER WHICH DAY YOU PICK, IT ALWAYS SEEMS TO BE WRONG

Some smokers choose their annual holiday to quit, thinking that away from the stress of work they'll cope better. Others pick a time when they've got no social events lined up and hope they won't be tempted. The trouble with these approaches is that they leave the lingering doubt: "OK, I've coped so far but what about when I get back to the stress of work?" or "What about that party next month?"

This is why we tell smokers to go out and handle stress and enjoy meals, drinks and social occasions right from the start. That way you prove to yourself right away that even during what you feared would be the most difficult times, you're still happy to be free.

So, how do you choose the best time to quit? Well, what advice would you give your loved ones? It's the same advice they would give you:

"PLEASE STOP NOW!"

You are fully prepared to quit. Like the boxer about to win the world title, you are at your peak **NOW**.

If you understand the nature of the trap, there's no reason to delay. If you're hesitating please go through the book again or call our free helpline.

YOUR FINAL CIGARETTE

If these three words conjure up images of a firing squad, remember it's not you who's about to bite the bullet, it's your nicotine addiction

When smokers think of their final cigarette, they often panic. It's like being faced with a "No Smoking" sign. They may be desperate to quit but still find the thought of never smoking another cigarette hard to accept. If this is you, don't worry about it; it's perfectly normal and natural at this stage and is no problem.

Most smokers arrive at our clinics in a state of panic which our method transforms into confidence and elation at the thought of being free. For some smokers it's unimaginable that they can get free. As the session progresses they go from having a fear of failure to having a fear of success as they realise that freedom is within their grasp. Don't worry if you have a similar feeling at this stage.

You had no need to smoke before you started; you have no need to smoke now. Lifelong non-smokers and ex-smokers, who make up the vast majority of the world's population, are quite happy without cigarettes. What is the pleasure? What is the crutch? If you've followed and understood everything, you'll come to the obvious conclusion:

THERE IS NO REASON TO SMOKE

I can't describe the utter joy of finally realising that you don't need to smoke. The relief is fantastic. It's like a huge, dark shadow being lifted from your mind. You no longer need to despise yourself, or have to worry about all the money you waste or what it's been doing to your health. You no longer have to worry whether you have a supply of cigarettes, or whether you'll be allowed to smoke, or whether the next person you meet is a non-smoker. You'll no longer feel weak, miserable, unclean, incomplete, guilty or trapped.

You will shortly be smoking your final cigarette and making a vow that you will never smoke another. Before you do, it's essential to be crystal clear that smoking gives you no pleasure or crutch whatsoever... and so you're not making a sacrifice of any sort. If you find the thought of never being allowed to smoke another cigarette difficult to take on board, try facing up to the only alternative: to spend the rest of your life smoking.

The choice is simple. If you still feel you're being asked to choose the lesser of two evils, ask yourself whether it would bother you if you never had flu again, or that you might never suffer from AIDS, or inject heroin? Of course not! So why should it bother you that you will never again suffer from society's No.1 killer disease? I promise you:

IT'S RIDICULOUSLY EASY TO STOP PROVIDING YOU FOLLOW ALL THE INSTRUCTIONS

You're stopping because you don't like being a nicotine slave. So stop thinking, "I must never smoke again." Start thinking, "Isn't it great! I don't ever need to stick these filthy things in my mouth again! **I'M FREE!**"

YOUR MOMENT HAS ARRIVED

Can you imagine how Nelson Mandela felt when he was finally released from prison? You are about to feel that euphoria.

I will soon ask you to smoke your final cigarette. Don't worry, it's natural to be a little nervous.

THE FINAL CIGARETTE

Often when we reach the ritual of the final cigarette at our clinics, someone will say, "I don't really want another, is it absolutely essential to smoke it?" This is a good sign, after all, the whole object of the exercise is to remove the desire to smoke.

However, loath as I am to suggest to anyone that they should smoke at any time, the ritual of the final cigarette is important for several reasons. This is a momentous occasion in your life, probably the most important decision you will ever make. You're curing yourself of a terrible disease and achieving something marvellous, something all smokers would love to achieve, something smokers and non-smokers alike will respect you for – and the person who will be most proud of you is yourself.

You're about to escape from the most insidious, subtle and ingenious trap ever devised. I've said any smoker can find it easy to stop and remain a happy non-smoker for the rest of their life, and that's true, provided you understand the nature of the trap. However, don't underplay your achievement as it takes courage to open your mind, engage in the process and then go for it.

You commit to being a non-smoker when you make your vow and you become a non-smoker the moment that you extinguish your final cigarette. It's important to recognise that moment and to stub out that last cigarette triumphantly: "Yes! I'm a non-smoker – I'm FREE!"

When you smoke your final cigarette, focus on it. Be fully aware of the vile smell, the disgusting taste, the filth you're breathing into your lungs.

After the first puff, look at the filter tip. Observe that it's already discoloured. Take the second puff through a clean, white tissue. Look at the stain on the tissue and think of your lungs.

Remember, you're achieving something wonderful for yourself and for your life. This is one of those rare occasions when you're losing nothing and making marvellous gains. You will not feel deprived because you're making no sacrifice whatsoever. There is nothing to give up. So banish any sense of doom or gloom and start off with a feeling of excitement, of relief that the whole filthy nightmare is now finally over and of elation that you are now free. Enjoy being a non-smoker right from the start.

I WOULD NOW LIKE YOU TO SMOKE YOUR FINAL CIGARETTE

For a few days you may sense the Little Monster's death throes as your body withdraws from nicotine. Smokers on the willpower method respond to these death throes in a variety of ways: feeling irritable, restless, bad-tempered, insecure, disorientated or lethargic. Of course smokers already suffer these feelings throughout their smoking lives; these are the feelings they interpret as needing or wanting a cigarette. However, far from worrying about the death throes, with Allen Carr's Easyway you're going to delight in them.

Although the death throes are real and physical, be aware that they're caused by the previous cigarette and will not be relieved by the next one. They're only noticeable over the first five days and then gone forever. There's **NO PAIN** and, provided you don't start to worry about it, or start to crave a cigarette, there's **NO PROBLEM**.

The fact that the withdrawal is so slight is good news. It means that it's easy to quit. However, the very insignificance of the physical aggravation can cause confusion for some smokers. They only identify the feeling as "I need or want a cigarette." If or when this feeling appears, it's essential that you stop thinking of it as "I want a cigarette" and start recognising it for what it is: the body withdrawing from nicotine.

Imagine you have a Little Monster inside your body that's searching around the desert for a drink and you're going to let it die of thirst. Instead of thinking, "I want a cigarette, but I can't have one", think, "This is the Little Monster demanding its fix. This is what smokers suffer their entire smoking lives. Non-smokers don't suffer this feeling. Isn't it great, I am a non-smoker and so I'll soon be free of it forever!" That way the withdrawal pangs become moments of pleasure.

Remind yourself that there's no pain and any aggravation you might be feeling is not because you've stopped smoking, but because you started in the first place. Also remember that another cigarette, far from relieving that aggravation, would ensure that you suffer it for the rest of your life.

Enjoy starving that Little Monster inside your body. Revel in its death throes.

Don't feel guilty about gloating over it; after all, it's been killing you, costing you a fortune and keeping you a slave for long enough.

WHAT NOW?

You should now be feeling great that you have smoked your last-ever cigarette. To ensure that you remain happy to be a non-smoker for the rest of your life, all you have to do is follow the rest of the instructions:

• Don't wait for anything. You are already a non-smoker from the moment you extinguish your final cigarette. You've cut off the supply of nicotine and unlocked the door of your prison.

• Accept there will always be good days and bad days. However, because you will be stronger both physically and mentally within no time at all, you'll enjoy the good times more and handle the bad times better.

• Be aware that a very important change is happening in your life. Like all major changes, including those for the better, it can take time for our minds and bodies to adjust. Don't worry if you feel different or disorientated for a few days, just accept it.

• Remember you've stopped smoking, you haven't stopped living – on the contrary, you can now start enjoying life to the full. Don't alter your lifestyle unless you want to anyway.

• Don't avoid smokers, or smoking situations. Go out and enjoy social occasions and handle stress right from the start.

• Don't envy smokers. When you're with smokers remember you're not being deprived, they are. They will be envying you because they will be wishing they could be like you: **FREE**.

• Forget substitutes. You don't need them and they don't work.

• Never doubt or question your decision – you know it's the right one. Never crave another cigarette. If you do, you will put yourself in an impossible position: you will be miserable if you don't have one and even more miserable if you do.

• Make sure right from the start that if the thought of "just one cigarette" or "just one puff" enters your mind, you think, "YIPPEE – I'm a non-smoker." The thought will pass very quickly and your brain will accept that it's trying to grow a tobacco seed on shiny, stainless steel.

• Never carry cigarettes with you, or keep them anywhere in your house. If you do, you open the door to doubt and almost guarantee failure. Would you advise an ex-alcoholic to keep a flask of whisky in his pocket?

• Don't try *not* to think about smoking, it doesn't work. If I say, "Try not to think about elephants," what are you immediately thinking about? It's impossible to make yourself not think about something. By even trying to, you get frustrated and miserable. Thinking about smoking doesn't have to make you miserable. It's how you think about it that matters. If you're thinking, "I mustn't have a cigarette," or "When will the craving go?" of course you'll be unhappy. But if you're thinking, "Great! I'm a non-smoker! Yippee! I'm free!" you'll be happy.

SUMMARY

- *Remember the checklist, RATIONALISED.*

- *The best time to quit is NOW.*

- *Don't skip the final cigarette.*

- *Read the instructions carefully – AND FOLLOW THEM TO THE LETTER.*

- *Don't worry about the death throes of the Little Monster – enjoy killing him off.*

- *CONGRATULATIONS, YOU ARE NOW A NON-SMOKER!*

"YIPPEE!! I'M A NON-SMOKER!"

CHAPTER 19

THE HYPNOTHERAPY

*Once you have read this entire book, followed the instructions
and smoked your final cigarette, the attached hypnotherapy CD will
help you absorb the method and ensure that you're happy
to remain a non-smoker*

Although hypnotherapy has always been used at Allen Carr's Easyway clinics, it's not the hypnotherapy itself that enables smokers to find it easy to stop, it's removing the illusion that they're giving up a genuine pleasure or crutch. Hypnotherapy can be a helpful tool in this process. However, to say that hypnotherapy can help someone stop smoking is as simplistic as saying that a book can help someone stop smoking. It depends what information is contained in the hypnotherapy or the book.

In this book, supported by the attached CD, you have received the proven method from the world's leading expert on stopping smoking. At our clinics and with this CD the hypnotherapy is an effective and relaxing way to absorb the method without distraction or interruption.

HYPNOTHERAPY – A CONDUIT FOR THE RIGHT MESSAGE
*Imagine you're a farmer in a very dry part of the world. You have
no natural water source nearby but fortunately a pipeline has been*

built bringing water from afar. Is it the pipeline that makes your crops grow? Of course not, it's the water that comes out of it. If the pipeline were carrying oil instead of water, it wouldn't benefit the crops at all. Hypnotherapy is similar to a pipeline. It's only effective if the content is right.

Visitors to our clinics find an environment geared towards relaxation and comfort: comfortable chairs, soft light, a pleasant temperature. All you have to do is sit back, relax and absorb the messages.

You might be apprehensive about what is often referred to as "going under", or being "put to sleep", or "losing control". Let me reassure you:

NOTHING WEIRD IS GOING TO HAPPEN

There is no danger or loss of control. Some people do drift off to sleep during hypnosis, and that's fine, as their unconscious mind will still hear and absorb the messages. However, the aim is not to fall asleep, simply to relax. You will remain in control throughout the hypnotherapy and there are no ill effects whatsoever. If an emergency were to arise, rest assured that you would respond as normal even if you have drifted off to sleep. There's absolutely nothing to be worried or concerned about.

You may experience a floating feeling, or a feeling of deep relaxation, and your thoughts may drift pleasantly as if in a daydream which can be rather enjoyable. Most people, though, report that nothing much seems to happen and all that's required of you is to be nicely relaxed and ready to absorb the messages that will ensure you remain a happy non-smoker for the rest of your life.

The content of the hypnotherapy CD has been tailor-made specifically for use with this book and is completely different from that used in our clinics. **IT WILL NOT BE EFFECTIVE UNLESS YOU HAVE ALREADY READ THE BOOK AND SMOKED YOUR FINAL CIGARETTE. IF YOU HAVE NOT ALREADY DONE SO, PLEASE DO SO BEFORE LISTENING TO THE HYPNOTHERAPY.**

CHAPTER 20

REACTIONS TO ALLEN CARR'S EASYWAY

Every day emails pour into allencarr.com from all over the world. Here are some examples:

After smoking 50 cigarettes a day for 20 years, I am finally free of their evil grip. My friend was told by his friend to read the book. He did, and hasn't smoked for 5 years. My friend told me to get the book. I did, and have been smoke-free for 4 years now. It was the easiest thing to do, the total opposite of what I had dreaded – withdrawal symptoms, weight gain, etc. My 4 year-old son will never, EVER see a cigarette in my mouth. I thank Allen Carr for my happiness and believe his method should be advertised on every pack of cigarettes!

Mike Gordon, London, UK

I read the book, and it is like magic. I can't believe it – I've smoked for more than half my life, just like my parents, just like their parents . . . The idea of quitting, of "depriving" myself of something every day for the rest of my life made me think I'd never be able to break free. And now, I love being a non-smoker. Something I thought would be impossible was easy, and I enjoyed it, and am enjoying it every day.

Helen Parker, London, UK

I didn't know what it was like to not smoke. I started at 11, and finally tried Allen Carr's Easyway at the age of 40. I haven't smoked, or wanted to smoke since. Smoking has become something that I used to do. It's not taboo, or an issue, or a problem if others want to smoke. I'm finally free. Thank you.

Victoria Colquhoun, London, UK

I quit about 2 years ago with Allen Carr's Easyway and felt so happy and free. I never had any desire to smoke. I never had any sense of withdrawal or being deprived. I had no problem going out for a drink with friends while they were smoking around me, offering me cigarettes, whereas that was always my downfall when trying to quit before.

Martin Byrne, Belfast, Northern Ireland

For 7 years I spent a small fortune on cigarettes, putting up with bad breath and countless other anxieties young people shouldn't have to put up with. I thought of myself as a stressed-out, under-confident person who would be miserable without my crutch. Now, thanks to Allen Carr's Easyway, not only have I stopped smoking completely, but I also look forward to each day in a way I never did when I was a smoker. I feel confident in every aspect of life now, and I can live the rest of my hopefully long life free from the slavery of that awful weed!

Jack Seymour, Surbiton, UK

Before Allen Carr's EASYWAY, I'd never voluntarily read a substantial book in my life (excluding ones from school). I not only completed it in a weekend, I found it compelling, and was so eager to listen and complete it and hear everything it had to say, I stayed up a whole night, reading the other 150 pages to the end, and indeed, took immense joy in extinguishing what I, thanks to EASYWAY and Allen Carr, know was my last cigarette! I was amazed at how it reinforced such obvious and clear principles and concerns, which as a smoker, I had been brainwashed to forget. I am now a confident non-smoker, and don't feel like I'm missing out. May Allen Carr have my eternal thanks.

Adam Richardson, Durham, UK

My husband, daughter, and myself all quit smoking after reading the book. We have been smoke-free for three years. It was so easy, it seems like a miracle. We have NO desire to smoke again. Thank you for making this possible.

L. Formisano, North Carolina, USA

I started smoking at the young age of only 10. For many years I have tried every possible product to stop smoking but with no success. On my 50th birthday my sister gave me Allen Carr's book as a birthday present. The day after my birthday, I reluctantly started reading the book, "the unwanted birthday present". Today I'm a very joyful non-smoker. I can only praise the Allen Carr method and wish that I knew about it 20 years or even 30 years ago. I wish that I could become a therapist and help to spread this wonderful message to all those poor smokers out there!

Neil Malan, South Africa

Hi Mr Carr! I m writing a paragraph about your book since it s my bible. I carry it with me as a reminder of what I was before and how good I feel today. Thank you.

Heidi Karppinen, Sweden

I started smoking at the age of 12. Now I'm 29 and I'm a free human being again. I always thought I was lost but I wasn't. Thank you for my life. I mean it. THANK YOU THANK YOU THANK YOU

Miroslav Kanurecka, Slovakia

I was a pack-a-day smoker for over 20 years. I have just hit the 6-month mark as a non-smoker. There are no words to thank you enough. I am buying copies for every smoker I know.

Juli Goldych, Florida, USA

Thanks Allen, I'm FREEEEEEEEEE!!!!!!!!

Jack Wilson, Sydney, Australia

ALLEN CARR'S
EASYWAY CLINICS

The following list indicates the countries where Allen Carr's Easyway To Stop Smoking Clinics are currently operational.

Check www.allencarr.com for latest additions to this list.

The success rate at the clinics, based on the three-month money-back guarantee, is over 90 per cent.

Selected clinics also offer sessions that deal with alcohol, other drugs and weight issues. Please check with your nearest clinic, listed below, for details.

Allen Carr's Easyway guarantee that you will find it easy to stop at the clinics or your money back.

JOIN US!

Allen Carr's Easyway Clinics have spread throughout the world with incredible speed and success. Our global franchise network now covers more than 150 cities in over 45 countries. This amazing growth has been achieved entirely organically. Former addicts, just like you, were so impressed by the ease with which they stopped that they felt inspired to contact us to see how they could bring the method to their region.

If you feel the same, contact us for details on how to become an Allen Carr's Easyway To Stop Smoking or an Allen Carr's Easyway To Stop Drinking franchisee.

Email us at: join-us@allencarr.com including your full name, postal address and region of interest.

SUPPORT US!

No, don't send us money!

You have achieved something really marvellous. Every time we hear of someone escaping from the sinking ship, we get a feeling of enormous satisfaction.

It would give us great pleasure to hear that you have freed yourself from the slavery of addiction so please visit the following web page where you can tell us of your success, inspire others to follow in your footsteps and hear about ways you can help to spread the word.

www.allencarr.com/444/support-us

You can "like" our facebook page here **www.facebook.com/AllenCarr**

Together, we can help further Allen Carr's mission: to cure the world of addiction.

CLINICS

**LONDON CLINIC AND
WORLDWIDE HEAD OFFICE**
Park House, 14 Pepys Road,
Raynes Park, London SW20 8NH
Tel: +44 (0)20 8944 7761
Fax: +44 (0)20 8944 8619
Email: mail@allencarr.com
Website: www.allencarr.com
Therapists: John Dicey, Colleen
Dwyer, Crispin Hay, Emma
Hudson, Rob Fielding, Sam
Carroll, Sam Bonner

Worldwide Press Office
Contact: John Dicey
Tel: +44 (0)7970 88 44 52
Email: media@allencarr.com

**UK Clinic Information and
Central Booking Line**
Tel: 0800 389 2115

UK CLINICS

Belfast
Tel: 0845 094 3244
Therapist: Tara Evers-Cheung
Email: tara@easywayni.com
Website: www.allencarr.com

Birmingham
Tel & Fax: +44 (0)121 423 1227
Therapists: John Dicey, Colleen
Dwyer, Crispin Hay, Rob Fielding,
Sam Carroll
Email: info@allencarr.com
Website: www.allencarr.com

Bournemouth
Tel: 0800 028 7257
Therapists: John Dicey, Colleen
Dwyer, Emma Hudson, Sam
Carroll
Email: info@allencarr.com
Website: www.allencarr.com

Brighton
Tel: 0800 028 7257
Therapists: John Dicey, Colleen
Dwyer, Emma Hudson, Sam
Carroll
Email: info@allencarr.com
Website: www.allencarr.com

Bristol
Tel: +44 (0)117 950 1441
Therapist: David Key
Email: stop@easywaysouthwest.
com
Website: www.allencarr.com

Cambridge
Tel: 020 8944 7761
Therapists: Emma Hudson, Sam
Bonner
Email: mail@allencarr.com
Website: www.allencarr.com

Cardiff
Tel: +44 (0)117 950 1441
Therapist: David Key
Email: stop@easywaysouthwest.
com
Website: www.allencarr.com

Colchester
Tel: 01621 819812
Therapist: Lynton Humphries
Email: contact@easywaylynton.
com
Website: www.allencarr.com

Coventry
Tel: 0800 321 3007
Therapist: Rob Fielding
Email: info@easywaycoventry.
co.uk
Website: www.allencarr.com

Crewe
Tel: +44 (0)1270 664176
Therapist: Debbie Brewer-West
Email: debbie@
easyway2stopsmoking.co.uk
Website: www.allencarr.com

Cumbria
Tel: 0800 077 6187
Therapist: Mark Keen
Email: mark@easywaycumbria.
co.uk
Website: www.allencarr.com

Derby
Tel: +44 (0)1270 664176
Therapists: Debbie Brewer-West
Email: debbie@
easyway2stopsmoking.co.uk
Website: www.allencarr.com

Exeter
Tel: +44 (0)117 950 1441
Therapist: David Key

Email: stop@easywaysouthwest.
com
Website: www.allencarr.com

Guernsey
Tel: 0800 077 6187
Therapist: Mark Keen
Email: mark@easywaylancashire.
co.uk
Website: www.allencarr.com

Ipswich
Tel: 01621 819812
Therapist: Lynton Humphries
Email: contact@easywaylynton.
com
Website: www.allencarr.com

Isle of Man
Tel: 0800 077 6187
Therapist: Mark Keen
Email: mark@easywaylancashire.
co.uk
Website: www.allencarr.com

Jersey
Tel: 0800 077 6187
Therapist: Mark Keen
Email: mark@easywaylancashire.
co.uk
Website: www.allencarr.com

Kent
Tel: 0800 028 7257
Therapists: John Dicey, Colleen
Dwyer, Emma Hudson, Sam
Carroll
Email: info@allencarr.com
Website: www.allencarr.com

Lancashire
Tel: 0800 077 6187
Therapist: Mark Keen
Email: mark@easywaylancashire.
co.uk
Website: www.allencarr.com

Leeds
Tel: 0800 077 6187
Therapist: Mark Keen
Email: mark@easywaylancashire.
co.uk
Website: www.allencarr.com

Leicester
Tel: 0800 321 3007
Therapist: Rob Fielding
Email: info@easywayleicester.
co.uk
Website: www.allencarr.com

Lincoln
Tel: 0800 321 3007
Therapist: Rob Fielding
Email: info@easywayleicester.
co.uk
Website: www.allencarr.com

Liverpool
Tel: 0800 077 6187
Therapist: Mark Keen
Email: mark@easywayliverpool.
co.uk
Website: www.allencarr.com

Manchester
Tel: 0800 077 6187
Therapist: Mark Keen
Email: mark@easywaylancashire.
co.uk
Website: www.allencarr.com

Manchester – alcohol sessions
Tel: 07936 712942
Therapist: Mike Connolly
Email: info@stopdrinkingnorth.
co.uk
Website: www.allencarr.com

Milton Keynes
Tel: 020 8944 7761
Therapists: Emma Hudson, Sam
Bonner
Email: mail@allencarr.com
Website: www.allencarr.com

Newcastle/North East
Tel: 0800 077 6187
Therapist: Mark Keen
Email: info@easywaynortheast.
co.uk
Website: www.allencarr.com

Nottingham
Tel: +44 (0)1270 664176
Therapist: Debbie Brewer-West
Email: debbie@
easyway2stopsmoking.co.uk
Website: www.allencarr.com

Oxford
Tel: 020 8944 7761
Therapists: Emma Hudson, Sam
Bonner
Email: mail@allencarr.com
Website: www.allencarr.com

Reading
Tel: 0800 028 7257
Therapists: John Dicey, Colleen

Dwyer, Emma Hudson, Sam
Carroll
Email: info@allencarr.com
Website: www.allencarr.com

SCOTLAND
Glasgow and Edinburgh
Tel: +44 (0)131 449 7858
Therapists: Paul Melvin and Jim
McCreadie
Email: info@easywayscotland.
co.uk
Website: www.allencarr.com

Sheffield
Tel: 01924 830768
Therapist: Joseph Spencer
Email: joseph@easywaysheffield.
co.uk
Website: www.allencarr.com

Shrewsbury
Tel: +44 (0)1270 664176
Therapist: Debbie Brewer-West
Email: debbie@
easyway2stopsmoking.co.uk
Website: www.allencarr.com

Southampton
Tel: 0800 028 7257
Therapists: John Dicey, Colleen
Dwyer, Emma Hudson, Sam
Carroll
Email: info@allencarr.com
Website: www.allencarr.com

Southport
Tel: 0800 077 6187
Therapist: Mark Keen

Email: mark@easywaylancashire.
co.uk
Website: www.allencarr.com

Staines/Heathrow
Tel: 0800 028 7257
Therapists: John Dicey, Colleen
Dwyer, Emma Hudson, Sam
Carroll
Email: info@allencarr.com
Website: www.allencarr.com

Stevenage
Tel: 020 8944 7761
Therapists: Emma Hudson, Sam
Bonner
Email: mail@allencarr.com
Website: www.allencarr.com

Stoke
Tel: +44 (0)1270 664176
Therapist: Debbie Brewer-West
Email: debbie@
easyway2stopsmoking.co.uk
Website: www.allencarr.com

Surrey
Park House, 14 Pepys Road,
Raynes Park, London SW20 8NH
Tel: +44 (0)20 8944 7761
Fax: +44 (0)20 8944 8619
Therapists: John Dicey, Colleen
Dwyer, Crispin Hay, Emma
Hudson, Rob Fielding, Sam Carroll
Email: mail@allencarr.com
Website: www.allencarr.com

Swindon
Tel: +44 (0)117 950 1441

Therapist: David Key
Email: stopsmoking@
easywaybristol.co.uk
Website: www.allencarr.com

Telford
Tel: +44 (0)1270 664176
Therapist: Debbie Brewer-West
Email: debbie@
easyway2stopsmoking.co.uk
Website: www.allencarr.com

Watford
Tel: 020 8944 7761
Therapists: Emma Hudson, Sam
Bonner
Email: mail@allencarr.com
Website: www.allencarr.com

WORLDWIDE CLINICS

REPUBLIC OF IRELAND
Dublin and Cork
Lo-Call (From ROI) 1 890 ESYWAY
(37 99 29)
Tel: +353 (0)1 499 9010 (4 lines)
Therapists: Brenda Sweeney and
Team
Email: info@allencarr.ie
Website: www.allencarr.com

AUSTRALIA

Queensland
Tel: 1300 848 028
Therapist: Natalie Clays
Email: natalie@allencarr.com.auu
Website: www.allencarr.com

Northern Territory – Darwin
Tel: 1300 55 78 01
Therapist: Dianne Fisher and
Natalie Clays
Email: wa@allencarr.com.au
Website: www.allencarr.com

New South Wales, Sydney, A.C.T.
Tel & Fax: 1300 848 028
Therapist: Natalie Clays
Email: natalie@allencarr.com.au
Website: www.allencarr.com

South Australia – Adelaide
Tel: 1300 848 028
Therapist: Jaime Reed
Email: sa@allencarr.au
Website: www.allencarr.com

Victoria
Tel: +61 (0)3 9894 8866 or 1300
790 565
Therapist: Gail Morris
Email: vic@allencarr.com.au
Website: www.allencarr.com

Western Australia – Perth
Tel: 1300 55 78 01
Therapist: Dianne Fisher
Email: wa@allencarr.com.au
Website: www.allencarr.com

AUSTRIA
Sessions held throughout Austria
Freephone: 0800RAUCHEN (0800
7282436)
Tel: +43 (0)3512 44755
Therapists: Erich Kellermann and
Team

Email: info@allen-carr.at
Website: www.allencarr.com

BELGIUM
Antwerp
Tel: +32 (0)3 281 6255
Fax: +32 (0)3 744 0608
Therapist: Dirk Nielandt
Email: info@allencarr.be
Website: www.allencarr.com

BRAZIL
São Paulo
Therapists: Alberto Steinberg &
Lilian Brunstein
Email: contato@easywaysp.com.br
Tel Lilian - (55) (11) 99456-0153
Tel Alberto - (55) (11) 99325-6514
Website: www.allencarr.com

BULGARIA
Tel: 0800 14104 / +359 899 88 99
07
Therapist: Rumyana Kostadinova
Email: rk@nepushaveche.com
Website: www.allencarr.com

CANADA
Toll free: +1-866 666 4299 / +1
905 849 7736
English Therapist: Damian O'Hara
French Therapist: Rejean Belanger
Regular seminars held in Toronto,
Vancouver and Montreal
Corporate programs available
throughout Canada
Email: info@
theeasywaytostopsmoking.com
Website: www.allencarr.com

CHILE
Tel: +56 2 4744587
Therapist: Claudia Sarmiento
Email: contacto@allencarr.cl
Website: www.allencarr.com

COLOMBIA – Bogota
Therapist: – Felipe Sanint
Echeverri
Tel: +57 3158681043
E-mail: info@nomascigarillos.com
Website: www.allencarr.com

CZECH REPUBLIC – opening
2016 Website: www.allencarr.com

DENMARK
Sessions held throughout
Denmark
Tel: +45 70267711
Therapist: Mette Fonss
Email: mette@easyway.dk
Website: www.allencarr.com

ECUADOR
Tel & Fax: +593 (0)2 2820 920
Therapist: Ingrid Wittich
Email: toisan@pi.pro.ec
Website: www.allencarr.com

ESTONIA
Tel: +372 733 0044
Therapist: Henry Jakobson
Email: info@allencarr.ee
Website: www.allencarr.com

FINLAND
Tel: +358-(0)45 3544099
Therapist: Janne Ström

Email: info@allencarr.fi
Website: www.allencarr.com

FRANCE
Sessions held throughout France
Freephone: 0800 FUMEUR
Tel: +33 (4) 91 33 54 55
Therapists: Erick Serre and Team
Email: info@allencarr.fr
Website: www.allencarr.com

GERMANY
Sessions held throughout
Germany
Freephone: 08000RAUCHEN
(0800 07282436)
Tel: +49 (0) 8031 90190-0
Therapists: Erich Kellermann and
Team
Email: info@allen-carr.de
Website: www.allencarr.com

GREECE
Sessions held throughout Greece
Tel: +30 210 5224087
Therapist: Panos Tzouras
Email: panos@allencarr.gr
Website: www.allencarr.com

GUATEMALA
Tel: +502 2362 0000
Therapist: Michelle Binford
Email: bienvenid@
dejedefumarfacil.com
Website: www.allencarr.com

HONG KONG
Email: info@easywayhongkong.
com

Website: www.allencarr.com

HUNGARY
Seminars in Budapest and 12
other cities across Hungary
Tel: 06 80 624 426 (freephone) or
+36 20 580 9244
Therapist: Gabor Szasz and
Gyorgy Domjan
Email: szasz.gabor@allencarr.hu
Website: www.allencarr.com

ICELAND
Reykjavik
Tel: +354 588 7060
Therapist: Petur Einarsson
Email: easyway@easyway.is
Website: www.allencarr.com

INDIA
Bangalore & Chennai
Tel: +91 (0)80 41603838
Therapist: Suresh Shottam
Email: info@
easywaytostopsmoking.co.in
Website: www.allencarr.com

ISRAEL
Sessions held throughout Israel
Tel: +972 (0)3 6212525
Therapists: Ramy Romanovsky,
Orit Rozen, Kinneret Triffon
Email: info@allencarr.co.il
Website: www.allencarr.com

ITALY
Sessions held throughout Italy
Tel/Fax: +39 (0)2 7060 2438
Therapists: Francesca Cesati and
Team

Email: info@easywayitalia.com
Website: www.allencarr.com

JAPAN
Sessions held throughout Japan
www.allencarr.com

LEBANON
Tel/Fax: +961 1 791 5565
Mob: +961 76 789555
Therapist: Sadek El-Assaad
Email: stopsmoking@allencarr.
com.lb
Website: www.allencarr.com

LITHUANIA
Tel: +370 694 29591
Therapist: Evaldas Zvirblis
Email: info@mestirukyti.eu
Website: www.allencarr.com

MAURITIUS
Tel: +230 5727 5103
Therapist: Heidi Hoareau
Email: info@allencarr.mu
Website: www.allencarr.com

MEXICO
Sessions held throughout Mexico
Tel: +52 55 2623 0631
Therapists: Jorge Davo and Mario
Campuzano Otero
Email: info@allencarr-mexico.com
Website: www.allencarr.com

NETHERLANDS
Sessions held throughout the
Netherlands
Allen Carr's Easyway 'stoppen met
roken'

Tel: (+31)53 478 43 62 /(+31)900
786 77 37
Email: info@allencarr.nl
Website: www.allencarr.com

NEW ZEALAND
North Island – Auckland
Tel: +64 (0)9 817 5396
Therapist: Vickie Macrae
Email: vickie@easywaynz.co.nz
Website: www.allencarr.com

South Island – Christchurch
Tel: 0800 327992
Therapist: Laurence Cooke
Email: laurence@
easywaysouthisland.co.nz
Website: www.allencarr.com

NORWAY
Oslo
Tel: +47 93 20 09 11
Therapist: René Adde
Email: post@easyway-norge.no
Website: www.allencarr.com

PERU
Lima
Tel: +511 637 7310
Therapist: Luis Loranca
Email: lloranca@
dejardefumaraltoque.com
Website: www.allencarr.com

POLAND
Sessions held throughout Poland
Tel: +48 (0)22 621 36 11
Therapist: Anna Kabat
Email: info@allen-carr.pl
Website: www.allencarr.com

PORTUGAL
Oporto
Tel: +351 22 9958698
Therapist: Ria Slof
Email: info@comodeixardefumar.
com
Website: www.allencarr.com

ROMANIA
Tel: +40 (0) 7321 3 8383
Therapist: Diana Vasiliu
Email: raspunsuri@allencarr.ro
Website: www.allencarr.com

RUSSIA
Moscow
Tel: +7 495 644 64 26
Therapist: Alexander Formin
Email: info@allencarr.ru
Website: www.allencarr.com
Crimea, Simferopol
Tel: +38 095 781 8180
Therapist: Yuriy Zhvakolyuk
Email: zhvakolyuk@gmail.com
Website: www.allencarr.com

St Petersburg – opening 2016
Website: www.allencarr.com

SERBIA
Belgrade
Tel: +381 (0)11 308 8686
Email: office@allencarr.co.rs
Website: www.allencarr.com

SINGAPORE
Tel: +65 6329 9660
Therapist: Pam Oei
Email: pam@allencarr.com.sg

Website: www.allencarr.com

SLOVAKIA – opening 2016
Website: www.allencarr.com

SLOVENIA
Tel: 00386 (0) 40 77 61 77
Therapist: Gregor Server
Email: easyway@easyway.si
Website: www.allencarr.com

SOUTH AFRICA
Sessions held throughout South
Africa
National Booking Line: 0861 100
200
Head Office: 15 Draper Square,
Draper St, Claremont 7708, Cape
Town
Cape Town: Dr Charles Nel
Tel: +27 (0)21 851 5883
Mobile: 083 600 5555
Therapists: Dr Charles Nel,
Malcolm Robinson and Team
Email: easyway@allencarr.co.za
Website: www.allencarr.com

SOUTH KOREA
Seoul
Tel: +82 (0)70 4227 1862
Therapist: Yousung Cha
Email: yscha08@gmail.com

Website: www.allencarr.com

SPAIN
Madrid
Tel: +34 91 6296030
Therapist: Lola Camacho

Email: info@dejardefumar.org
Website: www.allencarr.com

SWEDEN
Tel: +46 70 695 6850
Therpaists: Nina Ljungqvist, Renée
Johansson
Email: info@easyway.nu
Website: www.allencarr.com

SWITZERLAND
Sessions held throughout
Switzerland
Freephone: 0800RAUCHEN
(0800/728 2436)
Tel: +41 (0)52 383 3773
Fax: +41 (0)52 3833774
Therapists: Cyrill Argast and Team
For sessions in Suisse Romand
and Svizzera Italiana:
Tel: 0800 386 387
Email: info@allen-carr.ch
Website: www.allencarr.com

TURKEY
Sessions held throughout Turkey
Tel: +90 212 358 5307
Therapist: Emre Ustunucar
Email: info@allencarrturkiye.com
Website: www.allencarr.com

UKRAINE
Kiev
Tel: +38 044 353 2934
Therapist: Kirill Stekhin
Email: kirill@allencarr.kiev.ua
Website: www.allencarr.com

USA
Central information and bookings:
Toll free: 1 866 666 4299 / New
York: 212- 330 9194
Email: info@
theeasywaytostopsmoking.com
Website: www.allencarr.com
Seminars held regularly in New
York, Los Angeles, Denver, and
Houston
Corporate programs available
throughout the U.S.A.
Mailing address: 1133 Broadway,
Suite 706, New York, NY 10010
Therapists: Damian O'Hara,
Collene Curran, David Skeist

OTHER ALLEN CARR PUBLICATIONS

Allen Carr's revolutionary Easyway method is available in a wide variety of formats, including digitally as audiobooks and ebooks, and has been successfully applied to a broad range of subjects.

For more information about Easyway publications, please visit
www.easywaypublishing.com

Stop Smoking with Allen Carr (with 70-minute audio CD)
ISBN: 978-1-84858-997-1

The Illustrated Easy Way to Stop Smoking
ISBN: 978-1-84837-930-5

Your Personal Stop Smoking Plan
ISBN: 978-1-78404-501-2

Finally Free!
ISBN: 978-1-84858-979-7

The Easy Way for Women to Stop Smoking
ISBN: 978-1-84837-464-5

The Illustrated Easy Way for Women to Stop Smoking
ISBN: 978-1-78212-495-5

How to Be a Happy Non-Smoker
ISBN: 978-0-572-03163-3

Smoking Sucks (Parent Guide with 16 page pull-out comic)
ISBN: 978-0-572-03320-0

No More Ashtrays
ISBN: 978-1-84858-083-1

The Little Book of Quitting
ISBN: 978-1-45490-242-3

Stop Smoking with Allen Carr (with 70-minute audio CD)
ISBN: 978-1-84858-997-1

The Illustrated Easy Way to Stop Smoking
ISBN: 978-1-84837-930-5

Finally Free!
ISBN: 978-1-84858-979-7

The Easy Way for Women to Stop Smoking
ISBN: 978-1-84837-464-5

The Illustrated Easy Way for Women to Stop Smoking
ISBN: 978-1-78212-495-5

How to Be a Happy Non-Smoker
ISBN: 978-0-572-03163-3

Smoking Sucks (Parent Guide with 16 page pull-out comic)
ISBN: 978-0-572-03320-0

No More Ashtrays
ISBN: 978-1-84858-083-1

The Little Book of Quitting
ISBN: 978-1-45490-242-3

The Only Way to Stop Smoking Permanently
ISBN: 978-0-14-024475-1

The Easy Way to Stop Smoking
ISBN: 978-0-71819-455-0

How to Stop Your Child Smoking
ISBN: 978-0-14027-836-1

The Easy Way to Control Alcohol
ISBN: 978-1-84837-465-2

No More Hangovers
ISBN: 978-1-84837-555-0

Lose Weight Now (with hypnotherapy CD)
ISBN: 978-1-84837-720-2

No More Diets
ISBN: 978-1-84837-554-3

The Easy Weigh to Lose Weight
ISBN: 978-0-14026-358-9

The Easy Way to Stop Gambling
ISBN: 978-1-78212-448-1

No More Gambling
Ebook

No More Worrying
ISBN: 978-1-84837-826-1

Allen Carr's Get Out of Debt Now
ISBN: 978-1-84837-98-7

No More Debt
Ebook

The Easy Way to Enjoy Flying
ISBN: 978-0-71819-458-3

No More Fear of Flying
ISBN: 978-1-78404-279-0

Burning Ambition
ISBN: 978-0-14103-030-2

Packing It In The Easy Way (the autobiography)
ISBN: 978-0-14101-517-0

DISCOUNT VOUCHER
for
ALLEN CARR'S
EASYWAY CLINICS

Recover the price of this book when you attend an
Allen Carr's Easyway Clinic
anywhere in the world!

Allen Carr's Easyway has a global network of stop
smoking clinics where we guarantee you'll find it easy
to stop smoking or your money back.

**The success rate based on this
unique money-back guarantee is over 90%.**

Sessions addressing weight, alcohol and other
drug addictions are also available at certain clinics.

When you book your session, mention this
voucher and you'll receive a discount of
the price of this book. Contact your nearest
clinic for more information on how the sessions
work and to book your appointment.

**Details of Allen Carr's Easyway
Clinics can be found at**
www.allencarr.com
or call 0800 389 2115